GOLFING FOR CATS

'One of the major headaches with which booksellers are invariably racked is the astonishing intractability of authors. The division between these twin curators of our literary heritage is over which of the two syllables of the word "bookshop" is the more important. How rarely can an author be found who considers, before even setting pen to paper, the marketability of his product! How often has an author rung a bookshop to say: "I'm thinking of doing a book, what's the best weight to go for?" or enquired as the exact dimensions of the bookseller's most popular paper bag, so that something may be written to fit it?

Hopefully, *Golfing for Cats* will change all that. A new era of inter-literary co-operation, it is not too much to say, may well be dawning. For not only has this book been put together at the optimum size and weight, it also concerns the three most perennially popular subjects currently to be found on the bedside tables of the reading public, viz. golf, cats, and the Third Reich . . .'

From the author's foreword

' "Golfing for Cats" is a marvellously deft and funny book, catnip for Anglophiles.'

New York Times Book Review

His contributions to *Punch*, Idi Amin books and THE SANITY INSPECTOR have established that Alan Coren is one of the funniest writers in Britain today. The paperback publication of GOLFING FOR CATS follows soon after his debut as a children's writer. The ARTHUR BOOKS, published by Robson, are a superb new series of funny Westerns for children.

Also by the same author,
and available in Coronet Books:

The Sanity Inspector

Golfing for Cats

Alan Coren

CORONET BOOKS
Hodder and Stoughton

For Victoria

Copyright © 1975 Alan COREN

First published in Great Britain 1975 by
Robson Books Limited

Coronet Edition 1976

Printed and bound in Great Britain for
Coronet Books, Hodder and Stoughton, London
by Richard Clay (The Chaucer Press) Ltd,
Bungay, Suffolk

ISBN 0 340 20998 4

Contents

Foreword: An Apology to the Bookseller

One of the major headaches with which booksellers are invariably racked is the astonishing intractability of authors. The division between these twin curators of our literary heritage is over which of the two syllables of the word 'bookshop' is the more important. How rarely can an author be found who considers, before even setting pen to paper, the marketability of his product! How often has an author rung a bookshop to say: 'I'm thinking of doing a book, what's the best weight to go for?' or enquired as to the exact dimensions of the bookseller's most popular paper bag, so that something may be written to fit it?

Hopefully, *Golfing For Cats* will change all that. A new era of inter-literary co-operation, it is not too much to say, may well be dawning. For not only has this book been put together at the optimum size and weight, it also concerns the three most perennially popular subjects currently to be found on the bedside tables of the reading public, viz. golf, cats, and the Third Reich.

Unfortunately—but, then, one cannot have everything, all revolutions are by nature imperfect—it doesn't concern any of them very deeply. In fact, glancing through the material, I found nothing to do with golf, cats, or indeed the Third Reich. However, they are all there on the cover, which may well be enough: the majority of books sold are given as presents, and the givers, only too glad to have the rotten problem settled, rarely give more than a perfunctory glance at the dust-jacket. I cannot but believe that this book will find its way onto the bookshelves, not to say into the wastebins, of golfers, cat-lovers, and students of military history, in incalculable numbers. (These would be even larger had I managed to get 'Book of Records' somewhere in the title, but this proved to be impossible: *The Golfing Cat's Book of Records* runs cumbrously off the tongue.

Similarly, I have been told that even more books about fishing have been sold than books about golf, but *Fishing For Cats*, conjuring up as it did the vision of someone leaning over a bridge with a mouse on the end of a string, stretched, I felt, ambiguity to an intolerable limit.)

Why, then, I hear you ask, should I apologise to the bookseller, having bent over so far backwards, not to mention sideways, to please him? Well, it is simply that some confusion may arise, this book having been ordered in the vast numbers necessary to satisfy the giant trifurcated public for it, when it comes to putting it on the shelves: should it go under GOLF, or under CATS, or under THE THIRD REICH; or, indeed, under none of these? (There is, I quietly submit, a good commercial case for putting it under BOOKS OF RECORDS, but I shall not push it.)

I leave, I'm afraid, the decision to the bookseller himself. If he chooses to opt for the safest course, and buy three times as many copies as he would otherwise have done, I should prefer, in the interests of modesty and good taste, that the suggestion did not come from me.

AC

Today Stansted, Tomorrow the World!

The frantic attempt earlier this year to disguise Britain's Stansted Airport as Orly in order to confuse a hijacker was a panic operation. With time to plan ahead things will be very different in future

'. . . and if approached by the alleged hijacker,' barked the Chief Superintendent, 'you will say: BONSOIR, TOUT! QU'EST-CE QUE C'EST QUE TOUT ÇA ICI?'

'BONSOIR, TOUT!' roared the serried ranks of constables. 'QU'EST-CE QUE C'EST QUE TOUT ÇA ICI?'

'Or, if that is too much to remember,' said the Chief Superintendent, marching along the line of coppers, flicking at an epaulette here, a white Sam Browne there, 'you will merely say: ALLO, ALLO, ALLO.'

'I thought that was English, Chief Superintendent,' said a young constable.

'Only with a haitch,' replied the Chief Superintendent. 'You are right in assuming that ELLO, ELLO, ELLO 'as a haitch hon it, but the French ALLO, ALLO, ALLO 'as no haitch. Of course, the haitch hon ELLO, ELLO, ELLO is silent, since we do not want to go around saying HELLO, HELLO, HELLO like a bunch of pansy poofters, but nevertheless I wish you to think in French, and therefore when you say ALLO, you will remember at all times that it *is* ALLO and not ELLO. Is that clear?'

'OUI!' roared the constables.

'OUI WHAT?' shouted the Chief Superintendent.

'OUI, SIR!' shouted the constables.

'Garlic,' said the Senior Security Officer of the British Airports Authority. 'There's the nub. It's these little details. During the war, they were always picking up Richard Attenborough for having British matches on him, or similar. Tying his boots wrong, standing up for women in buses, asking for HP sauce on his sauerkraut. Your average wog hijacker may not be an intellectual, but he'll have been briefed on detail, you can be bloody sure of that. It is all very well having your stewardesses standing about with onions round their necks, or customs officers playing accordions, or police walking about with poodles, but it is absolutely essential to get the small points right as well.'

'Like black berets,' said Officer Hoskins, who was young and keen.

'What?'

'On their heads,' explained Officer Hoskins.

'Blackberries on their heads?' said the sso. 'Are you off your bleeding wicket, Hoskins? It was Carmen Miranda had blackberries on her head, son. He's not landing in bloody Rio de Janeiro! He's not coming down in Monte bloody Video!'

'I only . . .'

'Shut up!' said the sso. 'I have prepared a small emergency kit for issue to all personnel. It contains: garlic clove, one; horrible bloody Frog cigarette, one; snail, one; thin poncey moustache, one; and large wine-stained serviette, one. At the approach of a diverted aircraft, all personnel will open their cocoa tin, stick on the thin poncey moustache, crunch the garlic clove between the upper and lower teeth, tuck the filthy serviette in the collar, light the horrible bloody cigarette, and hold the snail in the left hand, giving it the occasional lick. Is that clear?'

'There's just one thing,' said Hoskins.

'Well?' snapped the sso.

'Suppose it isn't France he wants to land in?'

The sso stared at him for a long time. There was always one, he thought. In every organisation, there was always one.

'You will have heard by now,' barked the Chief Superintendent, 'that he may not want to land in France. In fact, it has been drawn to my attention that the majority of hijackers wish to put down in Benghazi. Why this should be so, I cannot begin to guess, having had the privilege of serving His Majesty in that very location, which consisted largely, as I recall, of lavatories

4

without seats and Italians running backwards. However, the terrorist mind is a devious object, and if he wishes to disembark in some pongy desert fly-trap rather than in the elegant boulevards of Gay Paree, ours not to reason why. Now, since half our divisional strength has volunteered to rush about, as soon as he arrives, in bare feet and dirty old sheets, offering him pictures of their sisters in a variety of bizarre North African situations, this means that the efficiency of the remainder can only be maintained if maximum flexibility and mobility is ensured, which is why the mounted division has been pressed into service. Now, if you will all dismount, gentlemen, we shall run briefly through the few Arab words necessary, imshi, bint, shufti, baksheesh, etcetera—it's a very small language, fortunately—and then perhaps we . . .'

His words were drowned in the crash and clatter of falling policemen. They rolled on the ground in a debris of caps and truncheons and whistles and notebooks and walkie-talkies and pencils. They cursed. They groaned.

The Chief Superintendent looked at them.

'To begin with,' he said, 'you will observe that of the various animals that are taller than the horse, one of them is the camel.'

'At the approach of a diverted aircraft,' said the Senior Security Officer, 'all personnel will open their cocoa tin, stick the shamrock in their buttonhole, light the horrible bloody clay pipe, hold the glass of Guinness in the left hand and the potato in their right, and lean on the shovel. Is that clear?'

'There's just one thing,' said Hoskins.

'Oh God,' said the sso.

'I was only thinking,' said Hoskins, 'the Cubans have been quiet for a long time, haven't they?'

'Black Power,' barked the Chief Superintendent, 'is a force we ignore at our peril.'

'LAY IT ON US, BABY!' yelled the constables. 'TELL IT LIKE IT IS!'

'Very good,' said the Chief Superintendent. 'Try not to chuck yourselves about too much, though. A drop of sweat here and there's all right, an authentic touch as I understand it from the manual, but you don't want to end up with a face like a Neapolitan ice cream and suspicious brown streaks all over your floral shirts. Also, I see I have to remind one or two of you that the straw hats are to be worn instead of your helmets, not over them. And if I may single out PC 308 for a moment, who seems to have fallen behind somewhat in this morning's training, the burnous, dark glasses and shillelagh should have been jettisoned before you blacked up, 308. In your present form, you appear to be a coon Provo seconded to the PLO.'

'Sorry, sir!' snapped 308.

'Man,' corrected the Chief Superintendent, wearily.

'Sorry, sir man!' said 308.

The Chief Superintendent sighed.

'Just hold the bloody banjo, 308,' he said, 'and keep your mouth shut, will you?'

The airport was prepared for any contingency.

Parts of it were under snow; or, rather, salt. Parts sweltered beneath the sunlamps cunningly hung in the cardboard palms, above the rolling dunes of demerara. In one corner, a stuffed yak stood with its feet hidden in plastic alpine flowers, although it had been pointed out to the Senior Security Officer (by Hoskins) that the exiled Tibetan was a committed pacifist. Airport and security personnel ambled about, some white, some black, some yellow (their eyelids sellotaped to their ears), and two, at least, red, who were carrying signed photographs of Jane Fonda and Marlon Brando.

In short, every area of potential militant dissent had been taken into account.

Almost.

At 2.38 p.m. a young constable rushed into the office of the Chief Superintendent.

'Sir! Sir!' he cried.

'For God's sake, 546, smarten yourself up, you're a disgrace to the Force!' snapped the Chief Superintendent. 'Do up your dhoti!'

'Sorry, sir, bit of a panic on, sir, Control say a chap's just hijacked a Trident over Gatwick!'

The Chief Superintendent leapt up, snatching his swagger stick.

'Right!' he cried. 'Bang on! Tally ho! What's it to be, 546? Camels, penguins, alligators? Wogs, consultants, Gay Liberation? Say the word, lad, and . . .'

'I was coming to that, sir,' said the constable.

'Well?'

'He's an Israeli,' said the constable. 'He wants to fly to Tel Aviv.'

'*WHAT?*' shrieked the Chief Superintendent. 'We've made no provision for *Israelis*, 546! They've never hijacked anything. You must have got it wrong. He must have said Quebec Libre! Or Scottish Nationalist! Or . . .'

'Tel Aviv,' said the constable, 'is where he wants.'

The Chief Superintendent looked at the constable, hard.

'There's one thing to remember when you're speaking to a superior officer 546!' he snapped.

'What's that, sir?'

'Wave your hands about a bit,' said the Chief Superintendent.

The Short Happy Life of Margaux Hemingway

'*Meet Margaux Hemingway, the biggest girl to hit the fashion scene since Twiggy. She's blonde, six feet tall, and a grand-daughter of the famous Ernest. "Modelling is a tough business," she says.*' – Daily Mail

YOU KNOW HOW IT is there early in the morning in Granada with the bums still asleep against the walls of the buildings; before even the ice wagons come by with ice for the bars? Well, we came across the square from the truck to the Pearl of San Francisco Cafe to get coffee and there was only one beggar awake in the square and he was getting a drink out of the fountain.

We sat down at an outside table, in the sun, and we looked at him.

'There is only one beggar,' I said.

Harry looked away. He unslung the big Pentax ESII with the 250mm Takumar and squinted up at the sun.

'There is a hard white light bouncing back off the stucco,' he said.

'It is going to be one of those days,' I said.

'Yes,' he said, 'it is going to be one of those days.'

Charlie came up and sat down.

'I would not use the big Pentax, old one,' he said. 'It will make the big clatter. It will frighten the beggar.'

Harry swung the ESII around and put his eye down it, straight at the fountain.

'I like to hear the clatter,' he said. 'I like this thing with the shutter. It is a man's noise.'

'Cojones,' said Charlie. He spat in the grey dust.

'I guess it is time for the girl to go,' said Harry.

'Yes,' I said. I got up.

The beggar looked up at me when I got to him, and for a moment I thought he was going to give me a fight. But I had the Schiaperelli voile on with the big black Gucci boots and the solid brass Akko buckle at the belt, and it held his eye for just long enough. I put my arm around his shoulders before he could move.

'Que cosa?' he said.

'Nada,' I said. 'Nada e nada e pues nada.'

Harry let go with the Pentax. Clack, went the shutter. Clack. Clack.

The beggar wriggled a bit, but I held him. We got a lot of good shots that day. They came out in *Vogue* and *Harper's* after that, and I looked very good, with all these brokendown houses in the background, and my dress flowing over the beggar, and the beggar looking damned Spanish, and all.

The extras came over the wall, and we could not miss them. Jimmy just sat behind the heavy Arriflex and the extras came over the wall, out of the old Mission, and Jimmy just pressed the button and kept on pressing it, and the extras went down and when they went down they stayed there in rather sad little heaps, like broken dolls, their skirts up over their legs.

I had to step across them, after that. They were all looking up at me, and their eyes were open, and they had these fixed smiles on their faces.

'For chrissake,' said Jimmy, 'hold up the goddam toothpaste!'

I held up the toothpaste.

'This is the one,' I said. 'For healthy gums and bright, bright teeth, this is the one.'

The American was early for the appointment. He came into the bar and he mopped his forehead with a spotted silk handkerchief and he walked across to a table and he picked up more nuts than he could manage and some of the nuts spilled out of his hand and he looked at the carpet for a long time, but he did not stoop to pick up the nuts.

He licked his lips after that, and he mopped his face again, and he walked across to the counter and on the way he knocked over a chair and he apologised even though there was nobody sitting in the chair and nobody to apologise to.

He asked the barman something, and the barman nodded, and pointed to me with a glass he was wiping, and the

American buttoned his jacket and unbuttoned it again and walked over to me. He was about fifty and he was going to fat and there was one bead of sweat in the cleft of his chin.

'I am Edward Mankiewicz of Mankiewicz Associates,' he said.

'I know,' I said.

'May I sit down?' he said.

'Yes,' I said.

'I did not intend to sit down at first,' he said.

'That's all right,' I said.

'At first I thought we might stand at the bar,' he said.

'Sometimes it is better not to stand at the bar,' I said.

'Yes,' he said. 'Sometimes it is better to sit at the table.'

'That is the way it is, sometimes,' I said.

'I will get straight to the point,' he said. 'I would like you to model the new range of Miss Mankiewicz Modes for spring.'

'I thought it would be something like that,' I said. 'I am sorry, but I have all the work that I can handle, right now.'

He took his hat off and fanned his face with it.

'I can offer you ten thousand dollars,' he said.

'That is a lot of money for a modelling job,' I said.

He put his hand on my knee. I could feel the moisture seeping through my Thai silk. You know the way it is with Thai silk.

'We want you very much,' he said.

I looked at his hand.

'So it is that way?' I said.

'What way is the way it is?' he said.

I looked at the hand again, hard.

'That way is the way it is,' I said.

He took the hand away, quickly.

'No,' he said, 'that is not the way it is. I was just being friendly. This is a modelling job.'

'You say that,' I said, 'but how do I know that it is the truth?'

He looked away.

'Because I have a wound,' he said.

'Oh,' I said.

'It is from the war,' he said.

'It is in the place of which we do not speak?' I said.

'That is the place it is in,' he said.

I looked out of the window. There were many strong young

men in bathing costumes lying by the hotel pool.

'I am sorry,' I said, 'I did not know.'

'Why should you know?' he said. 'The war is a long time ago.'

'There are times when I feel I cannot go on with the modelling,' I said.

'You must go on with the modelling,' he said. 'There is nothing any of us can do about the war.'

'Yes,' I said, 'I suppose so.'

The helicopter came and took Jimmy away soon after three p.m. It just came and took him away, and I saw him going up into the white sky. I could see the big Konikoflex 35mm poking out of the gunport for a long time. I knew Jimmy was on the end of it, but I could not see him any more, I could just see the sun winking on the big Konikoflex 35mm.

I started the climb up the big rock. There was one roped to me above, and one roped above him, and for a time I thought we would not be able to do it, and when the hole appeared in my tights and my hairpiece caught on the overhang, I felt that thing in me which we do not say but which is always there.

And then we came over the ridge, and the wind was blowing across the peak, and I could hear the helicopter hovering above us, and I looked up and I waved the bottle, and I shouted out:

'It's the right one, it's the bright one, it's Martini!'

And it was all right, after that.

You know the way it is in Pamplona. Suddenly everybody is running in the streets and there are flags and children and the big women in the mantillas and you get caught up in it and you drink a lot of the red wine and you forget what it is that you have to do in the afternoon.

We went into the bodega after the thing in the streets was finished because we had to talk about what it was that we had to do in the afternoon, and a lot of people came up to me to shake my hand and to have their photographs taken with me because there are always people who want to have their photographs taken with you when you are one of the big ones and they show these photographs to their families and they point to themselves in the picture and they say:

'That is me with the big one, it was taken on that day when

she did six straight cover pictures in the afternoon, Dios! but they do not make those any more who can do six straight cover pictures in an afternoon!'

So I was sitting there at the table and there were all the reporteros and all the fotografos and all the aficionados, and then there was another who came up to the table and stood there. It was an old one.

And I looked at the old one, who was not just an old one, but who had also been a big one, some say a great one, some say perhaps the greatest one of all.

'Welcome, old one,' I said.

'Go with God, young one,' said the old one.

'A glass of wine, old one?' I said.

'Perhaps you should not take a glass of wine with the old one, young one,' said the one who was my manager. 'They say it brings the bad luck.'

'I obscenity in your bad luck,' I said.

'Gracias, young one,' said the old one.

We drank a glass.

'Is it possible for me to assist you this afternoon?' said the old one. 'I could stand in the corner and be a fuzzy one. I do not expect to be a big one, any more.'

'It is not good for a big one to appear as a fuzzy one,' I said.

'It is true I was a big one,' said the old one. 'I was known as the thin one. But they do not want the thin ones any more.'

'Better that you go now,' I said, 'than that they see you as the old thin fuzzy one.'

'It is not easy, the modelling,' she said. 'Go with God.'

'No, it is not easy,' I said. 'Go with God, El Twiggy.'

On Behalf of the Great British People, May I . . . ?

As the 73rd Annual Conference of the Labour Party burst into thrilling life, a letter home went inevitably astray. Just as inevitably, it ended up in my in-tray.

Belle Vue Hotel,
14a Khartoum Villas,
Cricklewood.

28th November 1974

DEAR ENID,

I think I speak for all of us here today in the Belle Vue Hotel, Cricklewood, when I say that it is coming down cats and dogs outside; but, to introduce a more hopeful note, I am happy to be able to tell you that I have received certain assurances to the effect that brighter periods are expected from the west later which may lead to outbreaks of sunshine during the latter part of the afternoon.

Speaking, if I may, for myself, and I trust you will bear with me on this occasion, it will, I am sure, come as no surprise to you to hear that the journey down from Wolverhampton was a bleeding nightmare, pardon my French. Yes, well may you gasp and stamp your feet! I see, my friend, that you, too, have perhaps shared my bitter experience.

Standing stood there as I was, for something like two hours, I had much time to ruminate upon the state of Britain today. Who were these people, I asked myself, sat all over the compartments? By what God-given right did they occupy seating positions which, had they not been occupying them, could have been occupied by other people who, as a direct result of this unilateral action, were thereby forced to squeeze against the

13

wet window every time some bugger went off for a wee, not to mention coming back from the buffet car with three teas, one of which ended up sloshed all over a raincoat specially dry-cleaned for the occasion and in consequence of which is now not fit for our cat to sleep on?

How, I hear you cry, can it come about in Britain today, in, that is to say, 1974, after all that us in the Labour Movement have gone through, how can it come about that a man bound for London can end up in a siding at Didcot, with his hat on a rack going to Tewkesbury? Well may you ask, my friend!

We come now to the second item on the Agenda, the Belle Vue Hotel, Cricklewood. I think I speak for all of us here today when I say that the fried egg has been like a rubber beer-mat two mornings running. Also, and I speak in this context as one who has been attending Annual Labour Party Conferences for thirty-eight years, I have never before had a blackie walk past my plate and pick the sausage off it. May I here and now, at this convenient juncture, say that I personally as a long-standing member of the International Socialist brotherhood have nothing against our dusky brethren who are doing such wonderful things in Africa, where they belong, and I stand four-square behind the Government on the vile, yes, *vile* iniquities of the Simonstown Agreement.

But—and am I wrong to assume that I may not be entirely alone in my opinion?—does this automatically mean these people have got the right to force their way into Working Men's Clubs, borrowing our darts and all that that entails?

Let us return, if you will bear with me, to the events of yesterday, when I, in common with hundreds like me, repaired to the Central Hall, Westminster, for the opening day of the 73rd Annual Conference. I shall not voice the deep hurt I feel that it is not Blackpool this year, not the lovely elegant Winter Gardens we all of us know so well, and no pier, neither, as far as I can see; I shall not speak of the absence of whelk or winkle, or the fact that any attempt to sing in one of them gilded rat-holes what pass for public hostelries is met with an opprobrium from snot-nose toffs in suede boots what calls to mind the worst excesses of Peterloo, also Winston Churchill shooting miners.

No, leave us merely draw to your attention the fact that when your hon. delegate, hurrying to add his small voice to the great multitude at Central Hall, tripped upon the step and fell against a large person in a bespoke black overcoat containing a genuine live carnation, a person, I might add, smelling like a Maltese ponce from something what had obviously been put on with a hose, no expense spared, he looked up and found that said person was none other than a Cabinet Minister!

Imagine, if you will, the chagrin, I believe the word is, of your delegate when, expecting a warm fraternal greeting from one Socialist brother to another, he received instead: 'Get out of my way, you disgusting drunken oik, you are standing between me and the cameras!'

Is this, I ask, the way in which the Party we love repays the selfless efforts of dedicated members, grass roots members, who for thirty-eight years have been annually travelling the length and breadth of the land to put the resolution that 'This Conference, having due regard to those processes by which such deliberations arrive ultimately at the stage which they have not only reached but can be seen by all men of goodwill to have been reached, nevertheless and notwithstanding calls upon the Government as a matter of utmost urgency to (a) impress upon Her Majesty's Ministers, particularly those concerned, the urgent need for taking steps to improve the situation as it stands, and, furthermore, to ensure that past mistakes are not repeated; (b) relieve the burden upon those who unfairly bear it and seek at the earliest opportunity for some means of seeing to it that those who do not unfairly bear it at present do so in the not unforeseeable future; (c) do all in its power to maintain what has to be maintained but at the same time spare no effort to change what has to be changed, bearing always in mind that what has to be changed must be taken in the context of what has to be maintained; and (d) raise the minimum wage to £438 per week'?

Let us turn, for a moment, from this bitterness. All that is in the past, despite a dent in my toecap which my long experience tells me will not bloody come out, that's £2.95 up the spout, you do not expect when purchasing brand new footwear in which to represent your Constituency Labour Party in a fitting manner to have some great fat public school pig step on you, and that, I say to you, is the sort of person that wishes to drag this country into Europe and have prices rocketing and Italian foreigners pinching the bums of our women. Get your knees brown! I exhort the Party's right-wingers who would sell us down the Mississippi for a mess of pottage.

But there are more pressing things. Time does not stand still, nor the mountains pause in their courses. I would put it to you, as I have put it to that big Irish mare who runs the Belle Vue Hotel, Cricklewood, that for £1.75 plus VAT, a man has the right to expect more than a pork pie warmed up in its own cellophane and a spotted dick with a crust on its custard you couldn't cut through with a Black & Decker. I say now, as I said then, and when I spoke I seemed at my back to hear the ghosts of Keir Hardie and Captain Webb and all those other great champions of the downtrodden: 'Call that a dinner? If I gave that to our dog, he'd sick it up!'

My friend, the Irish question has been with us for many a long day, and for many a long day with us it will remain. I have every sympathy with those engaged upon that tragic struggle, but I have no hesitation in telling you now that the Irish people have brought much of their current unhappiness upon themselves! Unless they abandon the sort of attitude which, to cite a typical example, thinks that by ringing up its brother, a great filthy unemployed brickie who comes in from next door blind drunk and grabs officially authorised delegates of the Labour Party by the throat and bangs their heads, for instance, against the wardrobe, they will never achieve that lasting peace for which all of us here today hope and pray.

Nor can much hope be held out for that other great struggle of which we are cognisant of, unless the doctors shake their bloody ideas up. Did the late, great Aneurin Bevan dedicate his life to the principle that some Paki quack had the right to tell people who wore themselves out fighting to get to the front of his surgery-queue that, and I quote: 'What you are suffering from is a black eye, and there is no treatment for it.'?

Ho yes, friend, go privately, is what he was intimating, I could see it in his little eyes! Go privately, go to my smart private nursing home where I do all my abortions, and we'll have that black eye of yours fixed up in no time!

You see before you tonight, then, a typical member of the Labour Party rank and file, and, may I be permitted to say, proud of it. My hat may be in Gloucestershire, my raincoat may be streaked with tea, my shoes may be all trod to bits, my tie may be round my neck with the knot under my ear, my eye may be black, my stomach may be rolling, my wallet may be empty, I may be the victim of coons, Pakis, Irish loonies, hoity-toity probably homosexual Cabinet Ministers what have sold out everything for private gain, property owners, flash Southern middleclass layabouts, millionaire doctors, and corrupt railway officials in the pay of the entrepreneurial clique.

But my head is high, friend! I have no fear that the new dawn shall continue to come! We shall march on towards it, me and I, unwavering, uncomplaining, and unchanged! The hour is coming, and when it comes, it will demand the man! I shall be there!

Your esteemed husband,
Norman.

And is there Magpie still for Tea?

Lord Blake, Provost of Queen's College, Oxford, has blamed television for the decline in literacy and taste standards among undergraduates. – Daily Telegraph

THE MELLOW CLOCK bonged four across the grassless mud of Judas College quad, and the flakes of Jacobean masonry dislodged by its dying stroke had not yet floated to the ground before the square was filled with the throng of undergraduates hurtling towards the JCR television set for *Jackanory*.

The Senior English Tutor watched them from his first floor mullion, and sighed. Once, the quad had been a flawless stretch of emerald; but that had been many years ago, when even a freshman could read *Keep Off The Grass* without moving his lips.

A knuckle tapped upon his door.

'Come!' said the Senior Tutor.

The door opened, and a red-eyed face peered round it.

'Good afternoon, Cobbett,' said the Senior Tutor, 'sit down.'

'Sorry I'm a bit, you know, late,' said the undergraduate, easing himself into a creased fauteuil. 'I didn't want to miss the last bit of *General Hospital*, did I?'

'Did you what?'

'What?'

'Never mind,' said the Senior Tutor.

'It's where Doctor Armstrong is worried about what Staff Nurse Holland is going to say about Doctor Chitapo's wossname with that Student Nurse Stevens on account of him being a coon and her brother Jeremy that's hanging about with the one from the chip shop with the big knockers not exactly going a bleeding bundle on it all. I don't know what Student Nurse Stevens sees in Chitapo, I reckon she ought to have listened to Mr.

18

Parker Brown's advice, all these people coming over here, where's it all leading, right?'

'I'm sure I don't know,' said the Senior Tutor.

'There you are then,' said Cobbett.

'I thought we might return this session,' said the Senior Tutor, 'to *Hamlet*. You will recall that. . . .'

'I think we got a condenser going,' said Cobbett. 'All through *Emmerdale Farm*, they was dwarfs.'

The Senior Tutor looked at him.

'The revenge tradition,' he said, 'was a framework which. . . .'

'Werl, not *exactly* dwarfs,' said Cobbett. 'Normal bodies, know what I mean, but little legs. And in close-up, all their noses stretched out. And when they all went out to look at that cow with the rash on its thing, it was about nine feet long and its thing was practically on the ground, like a bleeding great dachshund. It could be,' said Cobbett gloomily, 'the tube.'

'You did read *Hamlet* this week?' asked the Senior Tutor.

'What? Oh. Oh, yes, I read it, all right. I mean, not every word, as you might say, but I know what it's about, don't I? I know the, like, gist. What a load of rubbish!'

'Ah,' said the Senior Tutor.

'But,' said Cobbett, inclining his head, 'a good title. I'll give you that. Crisp. Derivative, mind—*Kojak*, *McCloud*, *Colombo*, *Callan*, *Barlow*—but crisp. What's he a Dane for, though?'

'I'm afraid,' said the Senior Tutor, 'I don't quite follow.'

'That makes two of us,' said Cobbett. 'I can see where you couldn't put him in a wheelchair, I can see why you wouldn't want him to suck lollipops or have a glass eye or anything, I can see where you'd want him to have some sort of original gimmick, but a *Dane?*'

'He was a Prince,' said the Senior Tutor, lamely, not certain why he was saying it, 'he was a Prince of Denmark.'

'There's that,' agreed Cobbett. 'There's never been a royal cop series, I grant you. *A British* royal cop, werl, you might have got away with that. I'm not saying you wouldn't have got away with that. *Charles*, possibly. Not much of a title, but good locales, know what I mean? Good twists. You could have him tracking down a different royal murder every week, who threw Prince Philip off the royal yacht, who strung Angus Ogilvie up

19

in the Sandringham laundry-room, what was the head of the Archbishop of Canterbury doing in the Queen Mother's hand-bag, all that kind of thing, yes, I take your point there.'

'Oh good,' said the Senior Tutor, faintly.

'But a Dane,' said Cobbett firmly, 'no way. Unless he was nude: people expect Scandinavians to be nude, he could be the first nude cop. Not necessarily the first *royal* nude cop, I'm not saying that. Could be a very big puller, that. You could shoot the rooftop chases from below, where he jumps the twenty-foot gap, a lot of possibilities there. You remember in *Danish Dentist On The Job*, where the hygienist with the curly. . . .'

'No,' said the Senior Tutor.

'Oh, well,' said Cobbett, not without derision, 'all that read-ing, I don't s'pose it leaves you time for much. Anyway, all right, it's supposed to be the start of a Danish royal cop series, I accept that, it's a reasonable novelty—but what a plot! What a load of old cobblers, right? The murder gets done with this bloke getting poison poured in his ear, and then he comes back as a ghost. What are we watching, *Tom and Jerry*?'

'There has been much speculation,' said the Senior Tutor, 'on the wisdom of employing a supernatural device in a situ-ation which is so much more sophisticated than the retribution tradition from which it springs. In Thomas Kyd, of course. . . .'

'I'll just bloody bet there has!' exclaimed Cobbett. 'You wouldn't catch Kojak buying information off a walking sheet. Mind you,'—and here Cobbett wrinkled his pale face in painful thought, and began, slowly, to nod—'mind you, there's nothing to stop the victim coming back from the dead, if you do it right. They find him in this orchard with an earful of woss-name, and his heart's stopped and everything, but there's still this faint pulse in his brain, so they scoop it out and weld it to a lot of bionic arms and legs they've got, and next thing you know he's come back as the Six Million Dollar Dane, running through the castle at sixty miles an hour and squashing Claude's head like a ping-pong ball!'

'Claudius,' murmured the Senior Tutor.

'And him,' said Cobbett. ''Course, there wouldn't be much room in it for young Hamlet. You'd have to cut his part out.'

The Senior Tutor walked carefully to the window, opened it, and breathed deeply.

'If we might leave the mainstream of the plot for a moment,' he said, 'I should like to hear what you made of Act V, Scene 1. The gravediggers, the comic relief and parallel, the return to a. . . .'

'It's not what *I'd* call comic!' cried Cobbett. 'Two men in a hole, it's a dead pinch from *Steptoe*, you might get a spin-off sit-com series out of it, but I very much doubt it, all that two-men-together routine, it's old hat, it's Hancock and Sid, it's Bootsie and Snudge, it's not very 1975, is it? Personally, I'd have 'em sharing a flat, the two gravediggers living downstairs, say, and the wife of one of 'em living on the floor above, and they put this advert in for a third, and it's this girl, see, and—here, I just remembered, you know when we were discussing that one with the coon who does his old lady in, and I said it had a lot of comic possibilities? Well, how would it be if you had the gravediggers and the bird and their first wives upstairs in the one house, and you had the Othellos moving in next door? A sort of *Whatever Happened To Love Thy Wife Next Door The Second Time Around*, know what I'm driving at, you could clean up with a show like that. You've got the problem of what to do with Hamlet again, though, haven't you, unless you make him this comic nude Danish cop who's always rushing in starkers and arresting the wrong people.'

The clock chimed again, once. Cobbett sprang to his feet.

'Whoops, 4.30, *Yogi Bear*!' he cried. 'That's all we have time for this week, I'm afraid, it's been wonderful talking to you, thank you for having me on the tutorial, next time I shall have with me *Macbeth*, and. . . .'

'I look forward to that,' said the Senior Tutor.

'Yes, a cop in a kilt, it could spell the end of bald detectives altogether, and we keep his old woman in, *Macbeth and Wife*, don't you just see Rock Hudson and—oh my God, 4.35!'

His footsteps clattered on the ancient stairs, and he was gone. The Senior Tutor looked down from his window for the last time, watching his protégé disappear across the quad, into the gloaming, doing his silly walk.

Ouzo Pretty Boy, Then?

THE SUMMER SUN was setting softly behind NW1, silhouetting the fashionable Victorian terraces and winking off the brightwork of the myriad Range Rovers ranked outside the premises of their elegant classless owners, as I trod with eager steps towards my dinner invitation.

It being warm, many a casement stood open, revealing the laughing occupants bathed in the roseate glow of their serried Tiffany lamps and filling the evening with the happy sound of gargling plonk and jokes in Wykehamist French. Everyone seemed to be throwing a party! At the upstairs windows, even the children could be seen toasting one another in bubbling Schloer as they hung cleverly from their expensive Czech climbing-frames, their colourful little Tommy Nutter pyjamas making the eyes pop as they clashed gaily with the shimmering *Observer* wall-charts of the vanishing red man.

Such festivity! Such smart abandon! Such infectious effervescence! And behind it all, the sound of thirty different quadraphonic stereo kits at different stages of their thirty Scott Joplin LPs, a great plinking counterpoint to which, surely, the restless ghosts of Scott and Zelda danced.

I walked along, composing rubbishy purple passages in my head in the hope that somebody would buy them, and wondering whether the night could possibly live up to this early promise. Whence this sudden joy in a neighbourhood for so long sunk in trendy gloom? Had they all suddenly discovered a cheaper nursery school, or that mercury had vanished from the tuna's tissue? Had wheatgerm gone down in price and property gone up? Had the Bomb been banned, and *Deep Throat* freed?

At the end of the terrace stood my host's house, six floors of new beige stucco, like a tall biscuit; I leapt the steps between the potted bays, and rapped the T'ang knocker, and the door

swung back to reveal that reassuring throng of dirndls, dungarees, pre-sweatstained bush jackets, mascara-ed dundrearies,
nipples, and wing-collared Redford dress bows which guaran-
tee that this is where it's at, at least for the time being.

'DARLING!' shrieked a shriek beside me as I crossed the thres-
hold, and I felt my elbow clenched in a grip that has made many
a fascist police stallion rear in agony. 'How wonderful to have
you with us on such an auspicious night!'

I turned, to find my hostess's black beret more than usually
awry upon her ginger fright wig and her dark glasses matt with
condensation.

'Thank you for asking me, Suna,' I replied. 'I had no idea you
were inviting so many people. A small dinner party, I under-
stood, a quiet . . .'

'Ah, but that was *before*, sweetie!' she cried. I glanced quickly
towards her uncharacteristic élan. She is a lecturer in Star-
vation Politics, and normally dour. 'We asked you two months
ago. The world has *changed* since then!'

'The street,' I said, 'certainly seems unusually animated.'

'Everyone,' she exclaimed, and her unfettered bust shook be-
neath the anorak, 'is throwing a tziki and dolmades party!
There isn't an unstuffed vine leaf to be had anywhere in
London! Isn't it thrilling?'

'I see,' I said, for at last I did. 'You are celebrating . . .'

'. . . the end of the seven terrible years of neo-Nazi oppression, right! We can drink ouzo again, my darling, we have lifted
the embargo on mainland retzina! I ran out this morning and
stocked up the larder with authentic pasdourma, isn't it fantastic, made in Athens and we have refused to buy it since 1967, do
you realise neither little Dominic nor little Cordelia has ever
eaten it?'

'That's great,' I said, downing a glass of something which
looked like coconut milk and tasted like the bottom of a hurri-
cane lamp. 'Isn't that great,' I enquired of a passing under-
writer and Maoist, 'Gavin?'

'Great,' he nodded, 'but personally Greece is not where it's at
for me. I am heavily into Portugal these days.'

'Gavin is free to eat sardines again!' cried Suna.

'That's marvellous, Gavin,' I said.

He nodded once more, and blinked back a tear, and blew his

nose on the I Zingari tie that served for a headband.

'I'm throwing a sardine and tawny port bash next week,' he said. 'I hope you'll come. Right after that, everyone's going to Lourenço Marques for the weekend. I think we, you know, owe it to ourselves.'

'*I'm* just back from Corfu,' said a willowy girl I did not know but whose desquamating tan was littering her black velvet tuxedo like sleet. 'I only went for the day, as soon as the news broke. I was very possibly the first Camden inhabitant to enter free Greece. I went around telling everyone I was a Trot, just to test them, and nobody cared, they all cheered and put their hands up my skirt, it was possibly the most moving moment of my entire political life.'

'In a way, it has not been all bad,' murmured Gavin, gouging a forefingerful of taramasalata from a proffered dish. 'Portugal, I mean. My father laid a pipe down for me at birth, and I might well have started drinking it at twenty-one when I was too young to appreciate it, and here I am at thirty-three, with twelve years in hand.'

'How do you like *them* apples, Salazar!' cried his companion, a short girl in a University of Just Outside Pasadena tee-shirt, ripped-off jeans, and a diamond solitaire the size of a walnut.

'The people triumph in the end,' murmured Gavin. 'They always will.'

I eased myself away from them, towards the bar.

'Look,' I said to Suna's husband, who edits a Sunday supplement and makes his own macrobiotic ice-cream, 'I'm afraid I'm not much of an ouzo man, do you think I could have a sherry?'

'Right on!' he replied. 'Mind, it's lucky for you Nicos Sampson got the push. We were just about to pour our Cypriot sherry down the drain, when the news came through. And, of course, with the Spanish and South African stuff already hors de combat, as it were, for a moment it looked as though the whole broad canvas of sherry-drinking as we know it was threatened with disaster.'

'Don't be too sure about Spain, Lucien,' said a short bearded poetess. 'Franco is fading fast, remember. Naturally, we cannot be too sure of the full political complexion of Juan Carlos, but I hear from sources normally to be considered authoritative that

24

we may well be drinking the genuine de la Frontera article before too long! Not to mention returning to our little holiday nest in Benidorm, which we have been forced to let since 1936.'

'It's the bullfighting I miss,' said her wife.

Across the room, a group of copywriters were breaking plates in time to Theodorakis, who had taken up where Joplin had left off. Their wives were shuffling brochures, and I joined them.

'The world is our oyster again!' cried one with a literary bent. 'But how do we *choose*? Shall it be Rhodes. . .'

'. . . or the Algarve . . .'

'. . . or should we hang on and hope for good news from Madrid and Christmas in Tenerife?'

The girl from the University of Just Outside Pasadena strolled by, gnawing a kebab.

'Personally, I shall be returning to the United States now that the, like, dark night is over,' she said. 'I hope to rent a house in Malibu for the impeachment. I have had it up to, you know, here with Chester Square, but naturally I keep faith with my promise not to set foot on American soil until they have committed that bastard to Joliet.'

'I'd forgotten all about America,' said one of the copywriter's wives. 'Were we supposed to embargo things while he was there? I wouldn't bring it up, only I have a Corvette. And Yin and Yang both have cowboy suits. It never, well, entered my mind.'

I left them somewhat worriedly debating the exact place of the Hard Rock Café in the Republican spectrum, and was, the hour being late, about to slip into the night when I found my way to the door barred by a man sitting on the mat, with his head in his hands.

'Excuse me,' I said.

He looked up, and his face was streaked with tears.

'All too much for you,' I enquired tenderly, 'the joy?'

He sniffed.

'Joy hell!' he said. 'It's all coming apart. If Spain goes, what is there left to boycott? I thought about Chile, but what do we buy from Chile, who goes to Chile, who *knows* from Chile?'

I patted his shoulder, and stepped across him.

'There's an awful lot of coffee in Brazil,' I said.

On a Wing and a Prayer

'The largest known creature ever to have flown, an extinct reptile with an estimated wingspan of fifty-one feet, has been discovered by fossil hunters in West Texas. The creature had twice the wingspan of the biggest previously known pterodactyl.' – The Times

FROM A HOLE IN A ROCK just outside what was to become Seven-oaks, Homo Britannicus slowly emerged into the grey morning. A single snowflake floated down and settled on his forearm, paused, and dissolved among the thick, matted hair. He watched it disappear, his thin rim of forehead wrinkling.

A second landed on his broad flat nose. He squinted at it until it became a droplet, and until that droplet vanished.

'What's it like out?' called his wife, from the dark recess of the cave. H. Britannicus shivered.

'Bloody freezing,' he said. 'Also, promise you won't laugh, the rain is coming down in bits.'

His wife scuttled out, her lovely knuckles skimming the ground.

'What?' she said.

'Look,' he said. 'Bits.'

She looked at the snow, and she looked at the leaden sky.

'That'll be the Ice Age coming, then,' she said.

'Here,' said H. Britannicus, 'what's that grey coming out of your mouth?'

'It's coming out of yours as well,' she snapped. 'How do I know what it is, I've never been in an Ice Age before, have I?'

H. Britannicus shook his head slowly. Tiny Pleistocene items flew out of his thatch, and hitting the chilly air, immediately became extinct.

'What's it all coming to?' said H. Britannicus. 'Where will it

26

all end? When I was a kid, the summers we had!'

'I blame,' said his wife, 'the tool. All these bone needles, all these flint hammers, it's not natural.'

'Progress,' said her husband. 'You got to have progress.'

He tried to stand a little more erect. It wasn't easy.

'I'm off for a bit of a stroll,' he said. 'I'll catch me death standing here.'

It was just outside what is now the sub-soil of Canterbury that Homo Britannicus glanced up through his rime-hung eyebrows and noticed a figure shambling towards him. It had a pterodactyl on its arm.

'Morning,' said Homo Britannicus, taking a firmer grip on his club, just in case.

'Bonjour,' said the figure.

H. Britannicus raised his club slightly.

'What?' he said.

'Mah nem,' said the figure, 'eez Omo Gallicus. 'Ow eez eet going?'

'Mustn't grumble,' said Homo Britannicus. 'Where are you from?'

Homo Gallicus pointed behind him with his free hand, towards France.

'Ah 'ave walk many days,' said Homo Gallicus, 'wiz a proposition.'

'It looks like an ordinary bloody pterodactyl to me,' said Homo Britanicus. 'And what's that round your neck?'

'Wi call zem onions,' said Homo Gallicus.

Homo Britannicus reached out and felt one, cautiously.

'You'll never kill nothing with that, son,' he said. 'Too soft.'

'Wi eat zem,' said Homo Gallicus.

Homo Britannicus looked at him.

'It takes all sorts,' he said. 'What's the pterodactyl for?'

'Where can wi talk?' replied Homo Gallicus.

They found a small cave, and crept inside, and sat down. Homo Britannicus blew on his fingers.

'I wish we had a couple of sticks,' he said.

'What for?'

Homo Britannicus thought for a while.

'I'm not sure,' he said, at last. He nodded towards the pterodactyl. 'What about him, then?'

'In mah country,' began Homo Gallicus, 'wi 'ave no dinosaurs. Zer dinosaur eez—'ow you say?'

'Extinct.'

'Exactement! 'Owevaire, wi 'ave zer pterodactyl. You, on zer uzzer 'and, 'ave no pterodactyl, but you 'ave zer dinosaur, n'est-ce pas?'

'Just a few,' said Homo Britannicus. 'They're a bit bloody ropey, mind. Past their best, know what I mean? We've let 'em run down, werl, there's no call for 'em these days, is there?'

'Ah beg to diffaire,' said Homo Gallicus. He bent forward, and his black eyes glittered. 'Mah plan eez to mate zer Gallic pterodactyl wiz zer Britannic dinosaur! Wi will produce zer Gallo-Britannic pterosaur, mon vieux! Eet weel be zer biggest flying objeck evaire seen!'

'So what?'

'Zer Ice Age is coming, hein?' said Homo Gallicus. 'In an eon or two, eet weel be 'ere. Wi weel 'ave to find warmaire climate, or . . .' he drew a thick finger across his imperceptible neck. 'Wi cannot walk, eet eez too far; so wi weel climb aboard zer giant pterosaur—*an'wi weel fly there!*'

'Gerroff!' cried Homo Brittannicus.

'Also,' continued Homo Gallicus, unruffled, 'wi weel rule zer worl'! Everyone weel want one. Wi weel clean up zer pterosaur market.'

Homo Britannicus, to be fair, did all he could to fathom this momentous idea: he furrowed his millimetric brow, he scratched his craggy head, he sucked his great green teeth. But it was not until Homo Gallicus began to draw upon the cavewall with his easy, flowing line, that his partner-to-be was really convinced.

It looked wonderful, in the picture.

Over the next five years, the innumerable, unforeseeable technological problems came forth and multiplied.

For two years alone, the dinosaur and the pterodactyl could not be persuaded to mate at all, and the wretched co-partners were forced to stand by while the two halves of the project shrieked and bit one another. But in the third year, by a process of strategic starving, feeding, and cajoling, the message got gradually through, and the dinosaur fell pregnant.

Ultimately giving birth to an enormous saurian cylinder with six legs and two very small wings. It flapped these latter for a few impotent beats, fell over, and expired.

'Ah well,' said Homo Gallicus, 'back to zer cave-wall!'

Which was all very well, except that the family of Homo Britannicus was finding it more and more difficult to make ends meet: it was not merely that most of their breadwinner's time was spent in husbanding the animals involved, but also that those animals were consuming a vast amount of food. They were being saved from natural extinction only at the expense of the unfortunate hominids who had been forced to cast their lot with them.

'You never told us it would cost this much,' was how Homo Britannicus's wife put it, over and over again.

Whereupon her husband would flatten her with his club, a gesture which over the years was becoming less and less affectionate.

But towards the end of the fifth year (by which time the temperature had dropped to a constant ten below zero, and the emaciated families of the luckless inventors reduced to gnawing for nourishment upon the misshapen bones of past failed experiments), a small pterosaur was produced of rather pleasing proportions. Even more encouraging was the fact that when it flapped its large leathery wings, it actually took off, flew for a few yards, and landed again without breaking anything.

'It works!' shrieked the two Homos, hugging one another and dancing great whorls in the encircling snow. 'A new dawn is breaking!'

'Erk,' went the baby pterosaur. It opened its mouth wide. 'Erk.'

'Eet wants,' said Homo Gallicus, 'to be fed.'

For five more years they fed it, while it grew bigger and bigger. The cold wind that continued to blow through Europe having taken its constant toll, the vegetation was now so sparse that the family of Homo Britannicus spent its every waking hour in scouring the white landscape for pterosaur fodder, they themselves subsisting on grubs and bits of bark and anything else the pterosaur could not use.

'When will it be big enough?' they would plead of the manufacturers, 'when will it be ready? When will it all end? When will the miracle begin?'

And the manufacturers, by now mere hirsute skeletons themselves, would say: 'Soon, soon.'

And then, in the bleak autumn of the tenth year, when its wingspan had reached fifty-one feet, and its sleek giant body was consuming a field a day, and its insistent 'ERK! ERK!' had reached a pitch and volume that would start avalanches rolling a dozen leagues away, they trundled the Gallo-Britannic pterosaur out of its enormous cave, and announced that it was ready.

'Wi weel head West,' cried Homo Gallicus, 'to zer sun and zer fleshpots!'

Homo Britannicus clubbed his wife for the last time, tenderly.

'Back in two shakes,' he said, and gathering the mangy ratskins about his jutting bones, he and his colleague climbed aboard.

The great wings flapped, and the pterosaur lumbered down the runway in a trail of webby pot-holes, and took off.

The last thing they saw, before the freezing snow-clouds enfolded them, was the pitiful little knot of rags beneath, staring upwards.

They seemed to be praying.

It was warm in the place that was subsequently Dallas.

A group of fat, balding hominids were sitting around a triceratops-shaped pool, examining a roughly circular rock that Homo Texus was rolling up and down.

'I agree,' said Homo Oklahomus, who had made the trip especially to see it, 'it could be very big. It could be, like, very big indeed.'

'With the right packaging,' said Homo Arkansus.

'With the right packaging,' said Homo Oklahomus, nodding.

It was at that point that the sun was blotted out.

'What the—!' cried Homo Texus, letting the wheel roll from his fingers.

They leapt up, as the pterosaur came in to a perfect two-point landing, and ran across. Homos Gallicus and Britannicus jumped down.

'This is private property, buddy!' shouted Homo Texus.

'And this,' cried Homo Britannicus, 'is the Gallo-Britannic pterosaur! It will revolutionise travel, it will open up whole new experiences, it will . . .'

'The hell it will!' shrieked Homo Texus.

'Did you hear the goddam noise?' screamed Homo Oklahomus.

'My God! yelled Homo Arkansus, pointing a trembling finger, 'look at its damn droppings!'

'The environment!' howled the Americans, 'The environment!'

Whereupon, brushing aside the enfeebled European bonebags, they fell upon the hapless pterosaur, and beat it to death.

The Hell at Pooh Corner

From Christopher Robin Milne's recent autobiography, it turns out that life in the Milne household was very different from what millions of little readers have been led to believe. But if it was grim for him, what must it have been like for some of the others involved? I went down to Pooh Corner—it is now a tower block, above a discount warehouse—for this exclusive interview.

WINNIE-THE-POOH is sixty now, but looks far older. His eyes dangle, and he suffers from terminal moth. He walks into things a lot. I asked him about that, as we sat in the pitiful dinginess which has surrounded him for almost half a century.

'Punchy,' said Winnie-the-Pooh, 'is what I am. I've been to some of the best people, Hamley's, Mothercare, they all say the same thing: there's nothing you can do about it, it's all that hammering you took in the old days.'

Bitterly, he flicked open a well-thumbed copy of *Winnie-the-Pooh*, and read the opening lines aloud:

'"Here is Edward Bear, coming downstairs now, bump, bump, bump, on the back of his head, behind Christopher Robin. It is, as far as he knows, the only way of coming downstairs".' He looked at me. 'The hell it was!' he muttered. 'You think I didn't want to walk down, like normal people? But what chance did I stand? Every morning, it was the same story, this brat comes in and grabs me and next thing I know the old skull is bouncing on the lousy lino. Also,' he barked a short bitter laugh, 'that was the last time anyone called me Edward Bear. A distinguished name, Edward. A name with *class*. After the king, you know.'

I nodded. 'I know,' I said.

'But did it suit the Milnes?' Pooh hurled the book into the

grate, savagely. 'Did it suit the itsy-bitsy, mumsy-wumsy, ooze-daddy's-ickle-boy-den Milnes? So I was Winnie-the-Pooh. You want to know what it was like when the Milnes hit the sack and I got chucked in the toy-cupboard for the night?'

'What?' I said.

'It was "Hello, sailor!" and "Give us a kiss, Winifred!" and "Watch out, Golly, I think he fancies you!", not to mention,' and here he clenched his sad, mangy little fists, 'the standard "Oy, anyone else notice there's a peculiar poo in here, ha, ha, ha!"'

'I sympathise,' I said, 'but surely there were compensations? Your other life, in the wood, the wonderful stories of. . . .'

'Yeah,' said Pooh, heavily, 'the wood, the stories. The tales of Winnie-the-Schmuck, you mean? Which is your favourite? The one where I fall in the gorse bush? The one where I go up in the balloon and the kid shoots me down? Or maybe you prefer where I get stuck in the rabbit hole?'

'Well, I—'

'Hanging from a bloody balloon,' muttered Pooh, 'singing the kind of song you get put in the funny farm for! Remember?

> "How sweet to be a cloud,
> Floating in the blue!
> Every little cloud
> *Always* sings aloud."

That kind of junk," said Pooh, 'may suit Rolf Harris. Not me.'

'Did you never sing it, then?' I enquired.

'Oh, I sang it,' said Pooh. 'I sang it all right. It was in the script. *Dumb bear comes on and sings*. It was in the big Milne scenario. But you know what *I* wanted to sing?'

'I have no idea,' I said.

His little asymmetrical eyes grew even glassier, with a sadness that made me look away.

'*Body and Soul*,' murmured Pooh, 'is what I wanted to sing. *Smoke Gets In Your Eyes*. Or play the trumpet, possibly. It was,' he sighed, '1926. Jazz, short skirts, nightingales singing in Berkeley Square, angels dancing at the Ritz, know what I mean? A world full of excitement, sex, fun, Frazer-Nash two-seaters and everyone going to Le Touquet! And where was I? Hanging around with Piglet and passing my wild evenings in the heady company of Eeyore! *The Great Gatsby* came out that year,' said Pooh, bitterly. 'The same year as *Winnie-the-Pooh.*'

'I begin to understand,' I said.

'Why couldn't he write that kind of thing about *me?*' cried the anguished Pooh. 'Why didn't I get the breaks? Why wasn't I a great tragic hero, gazing at the green light on the end of Daisy's dock? Why didn't Fitzgerald write *Gatsby Meets A Heffelump* and Milne *The Great Pooh?*'

'But surely it was fun, if nothing else?' I said. 'Wasn't the Milne household full of laughter and gaiety and—'

'A. A. Milne,' Pooh interrupted, 'was an Assistant Editor of *Punch*. He used to come home like Bela Lugosi. I tell you, if we wanted a laugh, we used to take a stroll round Hampstead cemetery.'

Desperately, for the heartbreak of seeing this tattered toy slumped among his emotional debris was becoming unendurable, I sought an alternative tack.

'But think,' I said cheerily, 'of all the millions of children you have made happy!'

He was not to be shaken from his gloom.

'I'd rather,' he grunted, 'think of all the bears I've made miserable. After the Pooh books, the industry went mad. My people came off the assembly line like sausages. Millions of little bears marching towards the exact same fate as my own, into the hands of kids who'd digested the Milne rubbish, millions of nursery tea-parties where they were forced to sit around propped against a stuffed piglet in front of a little plastic plate and have some lousy infant smear their faces with jam. "O look, nurse, Pooh's ate up all his cake!" Have you any idea what it's like,' he said, 'having marmalade on your fur? It never,' and his voice dropped an octave, 'happened to Bulldog Drummond.'

'I'm sorry?'

Pooh reached for a grubby notebook, and flipped it open.

'"Suddenly the door burst from its hinges, and the doorway filled with a huge and terrible shape.

'"Get away from that girl, you filthy Hun swine!" it cried.

'"The black-hearted fiend who had been crouched over the lovely Phyllis turned and thrust a fist into his evil mouth.

'"Mein Gott!" he shrieked, "Es ist Edward Bear, MC,

DSO!"'
'"With one bound, our hero. . . ."'
Pooh snapped the notebook shut.
'What's the use?' he said. '*I* wrote that, you know. After
Milne packed it in, I said to myself, it's not too late, I know
where the pencil-box is, I shall come back like Sherlock
Holmes, a new image, a . . . I took it to every publisher in
London. "Yes, very interesting," they said, "what about put-
ting in a bit where he gets his paw stuck in a honey jar, how
would it be if he went off with Roo and fell in a swamp, and
while you're at it, could he sing a couple of songs about bath-
night?"'
He fell silent. I cleared my throat a couple of times. Far off, a
dog barked, a lift clanged. I stood up, at last, since there seemed
nothing more to say.
'Is there anything you need?' I said, somewhat lamely.
'That's all right,' said Winnie-the-Pooh. 'I get by. No slice of
the royalties, of course, oh dear me no, well, I'm only the bloody
bear, aren't I? Tell you what, though, if you're going past an
off-license, you might have them send up a bottle of gin.'
'I'd be delighted to,' I said.
He saw me to the door.
'Funny thing,' he said, 'I could never stand honey.'

In Sickness and in Health

IT WAS JUST THE OTHER DAY—July 10, 1984, to be exact—that I found myself limping through the august portico of the Royal Free Thomtholomew's College Hospital, London's wonderful National Health co-operative, in the hope of finding a soothing hand to bind up an ankle sprained the previous night in a nasty gin accident.

The casualty department was, as we who are fortunate enough to live upon this happy island have long come to expect, a model of efficiency: the injured had been neatly sorted into piles, each patient carefully labelled with his date of entry and next-of-kin, the polythene bags of dead hung on clever little pegs convenient to the garbage disposal, the Muzak had thoughtfully been turned up to drown the shrieks of the inconsiderate maimed, and the bright red carpet upon the floor had been brilliantly chosen so that colour took its correct priority over sterility.

I could not have been sitting there for more than a day or so when an attractive young boilerman came along, examined the number stencilled on my forehead, blew his nose on his apron and said:

'The Chief Shop Steward will see you now.'

Carefully stepping over two of my recent neighbours, a pair of road accident victims betrayed by weak-willed impatience into attempting to amputate one another's legs, I followed the nurse down a long dark corridor, no easy journey, given the difficulty of beating flies off while hopping on one leg, and found myself, at last, being shown into a comfortable consulting room that bore all the familiar hallmarks of senior medical occupancy: an elegant *Penthouse* calendar, a worn dartboard, a Bass dispenser, and an up-ended packing case at which four men in dungarees and rubber gloves were playing brag.

'Who's this, then?' said the tallest of the four. 'Your two quid, and up two.'

'786544,' said the boilerman. 'He's got a hobble.'

'Oh, has he?' said the Chief Shop Steward. 'I'll see you for a fiver.'

'But I thought it was free here?' I said.

'You speak when you're bleeding spoke to!' snapped the Chief Shop Steward. 'I'm talking to *him*. Christ Almighty, three fours! Werl, that's me out, you lot better get off and start operating.' He threw his cards down and turned to me. 'All right, take your clothes off, have you brought a thermometer?'

'I really don't see that that's necessary, Doctor, all I wanted was . . .'

The Chief Shop Steward narrowed his little eyes.

'You watch who you're calling doctor, son!' he barked. 'I happen to be css of NUPE, Head of this great hospital, also one of the country's leading caretakers! Some people,' and here he prodded my chest with such authority that I was forced to hop suddenly backwards, 'do not realise what it takes to be a great caretaker, son. The years of training, the terrible hours, all them mops to see to.'

'Forgive me,' I said. 'I didn't realise to whom I was speaking. It's just a sprain, a doctor would be perfectly adequate, I don't know why they bothered you, sir, I . . .'

'Everybody has to come through me,' said the css. 'Unless I'm certain it's a genuine bona fide case, they're out of here so fast their feet don't touch the ground! Or in your case, foot. Take your sock off, I'll get a quack sent up.'

He strode to the door, threw it open, shouted 'QUACK!' into the echoing gloom, and within half a minute we were rewarded with the clatter of scuttling boots, closely followed by a small panting man entirely wrapped in mangy fur, through the top of which his saffron face was peeking. He bowed to the css.

'Bugger me,' said the Head of the hospital, 'it would be bloody him!'

The doctor laughed, and rocked back and forth.

'He's a Lapp,' said the css. 'Can't speak a word of English. Some of our quacks have got a word or two, know what I mean, but your eskimo is a slow sod. Except when it comes to ears. He can't half take off ears, this one.'

'How is he,' I said, 'on sprained ankles?'

'Oh, he never touches legs. He's an ear, nose and throat man. And bloody deft. You ought to see him skin a seal.'

The doctor plucked at my sleeve, nodding his head towards the door.

'Tell him about my ankle!' I cried, somewhat urgently.

'Can't tell him nothing,' said the css. 'He'll do a marvellous job on your ears, though. Tomorrow morning, you'll never know you ever had 'em. He even fills in the holes. You're a lucky lad.'

'But there's nothing wrong with my ears!' I shouted.

'I'll be the best judge of that, mate! There's always something wrong with ears, fiddling bloody things, all them corners, real dirt traps. If I let you go away now, you mark my words you'll be back here one day, going on about earache and so forth, you have 'em off while you got the chance, son! You don't realise how lucky you are, he clocks off in half an hour, any later and you'd have had Doctor Ching, he removes kidneys by acupuncture, or tries to.'

I shook myself free of the Lapp, who snarled a little, but settled.

'Have you no English doctors here?' I cried.

The Chief Shop Steward stared at me.

'When was you last in a hospital?' he said.

'Oh, it must be, what? Ten, twelve years ago. Early 1970s.'

'*Ten years?* Bloody dark ages, son! Bloody oppressive yolk of Victorian wossname! Oh, they had English doctors, *then*, all right, poncing about in their three-piece whistles and laying down the law, taking organs out, sewing up people, sticking needles in all and sundry on their own initiative, no reference to cleaning staff, not a word to the car-park attendants, walking into operating theatres big as you please and up to their elbows in someone's innards without even a by-your-leave to the girls on the switchboard, you'd have thought it was Nazi bleeding Germany! Well, we couldn't have that, could we? We couldn't have democracy made a nonsense of and stand idly by, right?'

'I suppose not,' I said.

'A lot of our members was for hanging 'em outright, werl, there's always the odd extremist, know what I mean, but the voice of moderation was heard in the land, brother. Just scrap

38

the private sector, we said, that'll have 'em running off to America and Sweden and Holland and Australia and all them other places still suffering beneath the tyrannical heel of the quack, with a bit of luck it'll all be over by Christmas. 'Course, we were prepared to let some of the younger ones stay on, some of those on two-and-a-half grand for a hundred-hour week, nobody minded as long as they were making less than the cooks etcetera, also not interfering in the running of the hospitals, but they're a militant lot, your doctors, not to mention greedy and grasping, always on about more pay, no thought for the welfare of the country, know what I mean, self before state, it's what comes of not growing up in a trade union tradition, am I right?'

'Absolutely,' I said.

'So they left. Proved our point. If you want to get rid of private medicine what's occupying a monstrous almost five per cent of the industry, eroding democracy as we know it, robbing the individual of the right to choose to be indistinguishable from anyone else, making a farce of all that we have decided to call freedom, then it's no good mucking about with shutting a ward here, bringing a hospital to its knees there. If you want to get rid of private medicine, you have to go right to the root cause, right?'

'You have to get rid of the doctors?'

'Exactly! I can see you're not slow, son. Pity about that, I've got a nice position as brain surgeon going for a willing illiterate. Anyhow, after the English quacks all cleared off, we started attracting the right sort of people. You know, vets, pelmanists, masseurs, plumbers, and they tided us over until the foreign failures started to catch on to the wonderful opportunities. Like Nanook here, or whatever his name is, always wanted to be a doctor, so we put him through medical school, full six months course, and he's so grateful he'll do anything we tell him, as long as it's ears.'

'Ears!' shouted the surgeon, 'Ears!'

'Only word he knows,' said the Chief Shop Steward. He patted his head. 'You little treasure!' he said. 'Never have any trouble with him, never interferes, leaves the running of the hospital to them as knows about it, don't you, Nanook?'

'Ears!'

'You'll have to go with him, son,' said the Chief Shop

Steward. 'He can turn very nasty if he thinks an ear's getting away.'

'But . . .'

'Don't argue, son, he'll have a scalpel in you soon as look at you, this one.'

I turned, and hobbled out. Half way up the corridor, the Chief Shop Steward's voice boomed after me.

'You ought to get that leg of yours seen to, son,' he called. 'It won't get better on its own!'

Freaked Out with the Wind

'A civil war between America's young people and the established order of society—that is the forecast of the Presidential Commission on University Unrest.'—Daily Telegraph

SUMMER dusk was falling fragrantly across the arcadian sward of Tara College. Through the indigo gloaming, young lovers strolled, arms entwined, combing one another's beards tenderly and listening to the melodious hum of the faithful darkies crooning Mao's Thoughts on a hundred back porches. The evening air was sweet with the old-fashioned perfume of smouldering cannabis, and the velvet dark beneath the eucalyptus trees was punctuated with the stars of hopped-up glow-worms spiralling erratically on accidental trips. The ivy-covered ruins of Tara, that grove of academe almost as old as the decade itself and lovingly demolished piecemeal by succeeding generations of fond alumni, lay gilded by the sinking sun, dreaming its truly American dream. And on the magnolia-heavy stoop of the Phi Kappa Lenin sorority house, three svelte co-eds hammocked gently, pulling from time to time on the long cool glasses of lysergic julep and quietly losing their minds.

Scarlett O'Hara, most breathtaking of the three, was more than just the conventionally beautiful campus belle. True, the hand-cropped ginger hair, bushed into a winning frizz of Afro solidarity, sprouted modishly from her pallid skull, the lovely little eyes burned dopily from a web of pretty pink veins, the skinny white arms, blotched with attractive punctures, poked from her torn Che sweatshirt like pipe-cleaners, and her lovely legs, glimpsed through the holes of her faded levis, were as trim as a chicken's; but hers was more than mere traditional beauty. It was not for this alone that the male students of Tara fought, but for all those other qualities which focused in Scarlett to make her the quintessence of campus womanhood—the fluent Cantonese, the sexual ingenuity developed in a dozen South American guerrilla dug-outs during her Junior Year Abroad, the expertise of an arsonist of twice her tender years, her repertoire of political oaths, her ability to turn out a dozen Molotov cocktails in two minutes flat, her acid still, these were what raised Scarlett to that plinth at which young America grovelled and begged.

As she rocked there with her two beloved companions, a staccato, syncopated rattle shook the twilight.

'Heavens to Betsy!' cried Scarlett, blushing at the oath, 'what the **** was that?'

'That am mah people a-practisin',' murmured her friend Beulah. 'We calls it automatic fire!'

'It's certainly catchy,' exclaimed Scarlett, snapping her fingers.

'Yassum,' said Beulah, who had a Ph.D. in dialect, 'we jus' pick up any insterments the white folks leave lyin' aroun' and we jus' kinda extemporise.' She cocked an expert ear. 'That am a Voroshilov .50 hittin' de solo spot right now, heh-heh-heh! Back o' him he got a coupla Browning .303's and that's ole Mohamed X on the bazooka or I ain't no judge.'

The campus fell silent again. Small fires burned here and there.

'What rhythm!' sighed Scarlett.

'You better believe it, whitey,' cooed Elysia, third of the trusty trio, stropping a machete against her thigh.

'Oh, if only it could always be like this!' cried Scarlett. 'Surely this is what college is all about, lying here getting stoned, marking our own exam papers, running the faculty out of town, swopping lovers, cursing pigs, burning automobiles. . . .'

'Y'all cain't live in fairyland forever, Scarlett!'

Scarlett's hand flew to her bra-less bosom, knocking it hither and yon. That stirring squeak from the darkness! That glint of tri-focals in the rising moonlight! It could only be. . . .

'Rhett Butlah!'

The magic figure stepped forward, and the light fell on his

handsome face, wilting it slightly. The nocturnal insects nestling in his lovely beard, startled from their narcosis by the sudden brightness, hobbled dazedly out and took off. Rhett Butler, who had crossed almost an entire state on his moped, who had inhaled every known glue, who had left his imperishable political axioms on tiles throughout America, Rhett Butler who had fathered better than fifty per cent of the inhabitants of the Tara Soul Creche, was the archetypal campus hero. As he stood there, bowed by the weight of beads around his minuscule neck and wheezing sensuously from the exertion of delivering an entire sentence, he seemed to Scarlett to embody all that manly grace and subtle gentility for which their way of life stood. Ah, to be anti-married to this fine, balding, emaciated dwarf, who had burned down more libraries than most people had read books! But her body was already pledged to Ashley Wilkes, Beauregard Ginsberg, Robert E. Dunlap, the Tarleton twins, Stokeley Mgaga, H. Monroe Jefferson, and Wan Lee (Stonewall) Tong; and Scarlett laid great store by fidelity. She helped the dashing midget up the steps, and leaned him gently against the screen door.

'Why,' she exclaimed, 'what on earth do you mean, Rhett Butlah?'

'Ah mean,' he said, 'that we are on the brink of Civil War!'

They gasped.

'Our entiah way of life is threatened,' he continued. 'The Federal Government has mobilised! Right now thuh Union Army is preparin' tuh march on the deah ole Campusland and put an end tuh life as we know it!'

'But Ashley said theah would nevah be war!' cried Scarlett.

Rhett's proud derision struck the cuspidor and twanged off into the night.

'Ashley Wilkes, that no-good renegade! That traitah tuh the ole Campus!'

'Watch your mouth, Rhett Butlah, you are speakin' of thuh man ah sleep with Thursdays, a fine Campus gennelman who. . . .'

Rhett Butler laughed darkly and twirled his dashing earhairs.

'It may innerest yuh tuh know, Miz Scarlett,' he said, 'that your Mistah Wilkes has accepted a graduate trainee position with Gen'l Motahs—'

'No!'

'—and has departed for Detroit wearin' a three-piece suit, button-down shirt, and striped tie. He was last seen *talkin' to his fathah!*'

'That Ashley Wilkes done sold hisself out!' gasped Beulah.

'He'll get his,' said Rhett Butler. 'Thuh Campus Confederacy is already marshallin' its troops—ah am to be commissioned into Mao's Raiders, Miz Scarlett, along with thousands of other volunteers. We may not have thuh organisation and thuh money of thuh Union, but right is on our side, and thuh so-called President will find out he cain't interfere in thuh domestic affairs of the ole Campus. Why, he's even tryin' to break up the Black Panthahs!'

The trio gasped yet again!

'But they're *our* nigras!' cried Scarlett, tossing her flaming hair in a shower of comely dandruff. 'How dare he come down here layin' down the law about our nigras!'

Rhett popped a speedball under his handsome tongue, and grew grave.

'This war ain't just about the nigra question,' he said. 'Thuh Washington lackey is just usin' it as an excuse, to make thuh thing look like a Christian crusade. Thuh whole thing's a damn sight more important than the problem of our coloured folk.'

'How'd y'all like a hole in the head, honky?' murmured Beulah, drawing a Luger from her kaftan and slipping the safety.

'Don't take on now, Miz Beulah,' said Butler, trembling calmly. 'All I meant was that you people are just a part of thuh whole damn conspiracy—this war is about different ways of life, about industrial, urban, capitalist power on thuh one hand, and individual freedom, ole traditional values, and human dignity on thuh other. Washington wants to come down heah with its roads and its factories and its money and its pollution and all its disgusting ways of enslaving and corrupting decent people, and it wants to stop us screwin' around.'

'Mah family bin screwin' around foh generations!' cried Scarlett. 'Ah had six brothers dropped out already.'

'There ain't a Campus fam'ly that cain't say the same, Miz Scarlett. And we gonna fight tuh preserve our traditions, thuh

44

things what make us what we are: ain't nobody gonna tell me when tuh drop acid or stone pigs or smash windahs or dynamite thuh faculty-house. Anyone says different, he gonna get his haid kicked in. That's what civil rights is all about. Hey, looky there!'

They looked, and they saw: from all over the campus, the young rebels were converging, bearing torches, waving banners, riding anything they could lay their hands on, singing their time-honoured revolutionary songs to stir the heart and block the craw, thousands of young Americans in their raggedy uniforms and impromptu weapons, prepared to fight to the death.

It was difficult to believe that they had all burned their draft cards, once.

'It's beginnin', Miz Scarlett!' shrieked Rhett.

'It's beginnin'!' shrieked Beulah.

'It's beginnin'!' shrieked Elysia.

Scarlett O'Hara clapped her hands. It was so wonderful to see so many young men marching off to war. This was what America was all about.

'It surely is!' she cried, ecstatic. 'Ah wondah wheah it will all end?'

Rhett Butler turned upon the step, poised to plunge himself into history, a strange smile playing inside his beard.

'Frankly, Scarlett,' he said, 'ah don't give a damn!'

A Short Life but a Happy One

In which I learn to live with austerity . . .

'BRRRM, BRRRM!' I WENT. I spun the wheel, 'Ah,' I cried, 'the joys of the open . . .'

'Mind that cat!' shrieked my wife.

Just in time, I plucked it from my brown worsted, and threw it out of the car window. Another second, and the ginger hairs would have spread across the slick sheen of the vintage lapel which, after twenty years or more, will not take another cleaning.

'The joys, as I was saying,' I said, 'of the open garage! No carcinogenic reek of petrol, only the evocative pong of the mildewed banjo hanging high on the noonday wall! No money draining from the exhaust in some meaningless traffic jam gummed to the Southend Arterial, only the full exploitation of our mortgage repayments by sitting here on our nearly-own premises! No risk to life and limb from rusted automotive innards or roadhogging loonies, only the pristine motoring thrill, long gone with Kaye Don and the Prince of Wales, of being the only car on the road! Why, we have seen nothing all day except that old fridge in the corner over there and, on the horizon, that galvanised bathload of hibernating dahlias!' I changed gear, silently, smoothly, without even using the clutch-pedal, a skill I had long sought but which, until the death of petrol and the concomitant motionlessness, had ever eluded me. I glanced in my driving mirror at the children. 'Anyone feel sick?' I cried.

'No.'

'You see!' I shouted, above the roar of the engine (it being my wife's turn to brrrm), 'You see! Was Mr Heath not right (when

46

is he not?) about the hidden joys of self-denial? Beyond the pulling together, beyond the sense of pride in standing at the collective national helm, beyond the upshoring of our great environment, lies so much more, such as not having to crouch in crowded lay-bys scraping used breakfast off the carpeting with a tyre-lever for the world's derision. Thinking of which,' and here, one-wristed like an Arkansas bootlegger ducking the pursuing revenuers, I put the car into what would have been a screaming 5G turn, 'let's stop for lunch.'

I braked pointlessly, and we got out and flexed our limbs, and the children ran around the car, free of the risk of winding up in some juggernaut's radial tread and being stencilled across Europe. I looked at my own tyres: they were flat, and it didn't matter. The road fund licence had run out, and that didn't matter, either. The cat sat on the bonnet, as in the more advanced spelling-books, and the little ones sang for the joy of it: they have always wanted to take the cat on picnics, but, like most cats, it has always had things it would rather do than go for a ride in a car, such as tearing out the throat of anyone who tries to make it.

My wife opened the hamper, and we sat down (and how many picnic spots can you name which provide old armchairs whose quaint seeping horsehair so suits the rustic environs?) to a light lunch of fresh-peppered Ryvita and mushrooms newly scraped from the fractured damp course. How we both have profited physically from the shortage of everything edible! No overweight problems for us, and what a saving in clothes! Why, I can now, when a cold snap threatens, get both hands in one glove and, should it come on to rain, I merely crouch snugly beneath my walking stick until the dark clouds pass. Lest some spry conservationist leap to the complaint that there is a tree shortage on and that my walking stick, in addition to raping Mother Nature, has also deprived generations yet unborn of invaluable coal and its derivatives, let me just say that the item was built by me entirely from used matches. I have that sort of time on my lucky hands, now that there is electricity neither for tellies nor to read by, and I hope soon to finish my latest oeuvre, St. Paul's Cathedral. And indeed, if mortgages don't come down, move into it. We may have to crouch a little, but it is a price worth paying.

Si monumentum requiris, circumspice.

After lunch, we spent a gay few minutes romping on our hands and knees for crumbs and stalks (which, washed and dried, make wonderful crumb-and-stalk fritters) and, the supper problem having been solved, we walked out of the garage door and into the front garden, put the cat on the lawn next to my small daughter's panda and, as a sparrow winged its exotic way above the pair, we might have been at Whipsnade. Or, indeed, given a dolphin or two, the fabulous Berliner Tiergarten. Afterwards, still tingling, we strolled across to a neighbour's and looked at his dried-egg packet; our families are having Christmas dinner together, but rest assured that it was not suspicion that he might have jumped the gun which occasioned the visit (he is a good man), but merely to give the children something to dream about. We found the household torn, as so many are these days, between tragedy and joy: a shortage of ants' eggs (people, despite Government pleas, have been hoarding ants) had brought about the death of their malnutrited guppy; but, my neighbour being the enterprising and deft-fingered man he is, he was smoking it over a candle-stub he had won in a Savoy tombola. He put a finger to his lips as we entered; it was, he whispered, his wedding anniversary next month, and the fish was a surprise for his wife. We went upstairs to listen to his radio; the battery is almost gone now, but by holding the apparatus to the ear, one can hear a low nostalgic crackling, not unlike Vera Lynn.

It was all such fun, I hardly noticed the time fly. When I next glanced at my watch, it was half-past six. Mind you, it is always half-past six, the watch having long ago seized up as a result of the oil shortage, but I knew that the time must have been close to that, in fact, since, glancing through the window, I could see the evening paper being delivered. It was being delivered by no less a person than the editor himself, in a loud and penetrating voice, a practice into which he has been forced by the dire newsprint shortage. For a time, he would actually read aloud from the one copy they used to manage to run off, but when the last of that meagre and jealously hoarded supply ran out, he took to cycling the London streets on his auntie's Rudge, shouting the news through a megaphone, not unlike a rowing coach. We have always taken the *Evening Standard*, but receiving the news

48

two months late (three months, on one occasion, due to the waiting list on a brake-block) is beginning to tell, and we may shift allegiances to the *Evening News*, which has a larger circulation, the editor having taught his deputy to ride a horse.

So it was the children's bathtime, and back to our own home. It was pitch dark when we arrived, so it was fortunate indeed that the cat was with us, although the latter stages of the journey were marred by having to follow it through hedges in search of the mice which now form the main part of his diet.

And ours. If there is one thing which has slightly soiled the pleasure of austerity, and I mean no disrespect to our great leader, it has been the degradation attendant upon fighting under a hedge with one's own moggy for the prize of an emaciated rat-leg.

The children stood in the empty bath for a while, beating one another to a healthy glow with the dry loofahs while I played *Fingal's Cave* on a hand-wound gramophone and my wife did a realistic impression of soap, and when they were tucked up (we find a cat in a sock is a wonderful substitute for a hot water-bottle, if marginally noisier), we crept downstairs for that part of the evening we call our own.

There is always so much to do, then. Sometimes, we play quiz games; she, for example, will say 'Milk bottle' and then I will try to describe it, or we try to see which of us can finish spelling 'beef' without screaming or banging our head on the fender; sometimes, we'll dance in the romantic glow of our luminous alarm clock, or, if it's rained and our lips are moist, whistle a bit of Mahler; sometimes, when we feel less energetic, we take down our collection of pressed flowers and feel it together. We may have to stop that, though—I noticed, just the other night, that we seemed to be several examples short.

And I could almost have sworn I heard her crunching.

The Heathrow Tales

Whan that Aprille with his taxe-formes drere
Comes, draggynge in a new fynancial yeere,
Thenne many folke loke round to see how theye
May kepe the Inlande Revenue atte baye;
And hardly has the litel month begunne
Thanne journalystes start trekkinge to the sunne,
To write of places off the beaten trackes,
And sette expenses off agaynst thir taxe:
A pilgrimage, in shorte, not for their soules,
But (as it is wyth modern mankynde's goales)
To kepe a few bob backe. Thus, did I wende
To Heathrowe, there my further steppes to bende
Towards some sunsoked costa; and I founde
The spotte was thikke wyth pilgrims! All arounde
They milled and chattered, singlie and in groupes;
And everywhere, the bright-emblazon'd troops
Of Travail Agents hopped and chyrped like sparrowes,
Dyspensing labels, poyntinge uppe at arrowes,
Dyscharging these to Lourdes, and those to Rome,
And others who were off to see the home
Inne wich Lorde Byron lived, or John Keates died,
Or Wolfgang Amadeus Mozart cryed
When (being seven) his Daddye would not lette
Him staye uppe to compose a stringe quartette.
And yette, for all the bustle and the cryes,
Not one soule saw I takynge to the skyes,
And eek my own flyte no man came to call;
We merely mobbed the grate departure hall
And gayzed uppe at the indicator-bord,
For such bleeke gleenings as it would afforde
Of flytes not inne, not oute, not onne, not knowne,
Of strykes and goe-slowes; and muche else (not showne)

Like drunken crewes, lost rear doors, and the sounde
Of tickynge baggage, kept us onne the grounde.

Thus was it thatte it came aboute by chance
As we poore pilgrims trodde our loanly dance
Upon the Heathrowe tiles, thatte one of us
(Drop't there two dayes bifor by airporte bus)
Suggested thatte we wile away the time
With tales thatte eech wold tell the reste, in ryme!
We clap't, we cheer'd, our weery eyes grew bryte;
We sang the praises of thatte worthie wight!
Then satte we downe, wyth whiskey, beere, and gin,
And wayted for the firste one to biginne.
But lette me, whyle I have the tyme and space,
Ere thatte I ferther in this storie pace,
Sette downe the manere of thatte companye,
And wich they weren, and of what degree;
And eek in what array thatte they were inne!
And at a clericke wol I firste biginne.

A BISHOPPE hadde we wyth us in thatte place,
A slimme yung manne whose bryte and beerdlesse face
Glowed wyth a pinkish-white cherubicke hue,
Broughte on in parte by prayer, but most by Brut.
This worthie manne had turned his mohaired backe
Upon the easeful parishe life: no hacke
For Christ was he, to pat the wrinkled hande
Of borynge windowes, or each weeke to stande
Inne some raine-sodden pulpytte, there to speeke
Some low-paid sermon to the grottie meeke.
Westward he turned his course, towardes those isles
Where heathen soules pursued those living-stiles
Thatte frighte the Christian; where the idle rich
Have found atte laste a litel taxe-free niche
Whereinne to set thir golden calves; to pounce
Whenne golde goes up to ninety-five an ounce,
And where, to ease thir soules, they oft invite
The better class of prieste to spende the nyghte;
Or three months, if the truth were told. So thatte
They ease thir conscience, as we worm a catte.

The prieste in his turn, for the boone thus given,
Makes sure the taxe-evaded soule is shriven,
And coming home all tanned, white teeth a-gleem,
Turns out for cricket wyth his village teeme—
Hee fyndes the countryside the place to dwell;
For theologians writing *What Is Hell?*
(A six-part series for the *Sunday Tymes*)
Need peace and quiet; rural life, too, chimes
Wyth tearynge uppe to towne one day a weeke
So thatte the national presse may heer him speeke
His piece on porno in the House of Lordes,
Or rayle on telly about Christian frauds.

Biside him satte a NOVELISTE, al pale,
Who once, tenne yeeres bifor, had writ a tale
So true, so deepe, so geered to thisse darke age
Thatte, ere the reeder turned the final page,
He knew *Roome Atte The Botom* was the one
To acte on Eng. Lit. lyke the mornynge sunne,
Who sheddes his warmynge beemes on soggie soyle
To maturate the plottes where seedlynges toyle.
Thus, al arounde, we saw the seedlynges bask;
The noveliste, meenwile, clove to his taske,
And lo! Ere yet a litel yeere had trip't
He hadde terned out a stunnynge movie scripte
Based onne the boke. It won sixteene awardes
(And, naturally, reeped other fatte rewardes:
The noveliste moved to the South of France).
The nexte yeere saw a wonderful new dance,
The Botom (fromme the musical), by wich
The noveliste now waxed exceedynge rich.
And still the grate creative juices flow'd!
For, after thatte, thisse noveliste now show'd
How righte *Roome Atte The Botom* prov'd to bee
In ninety-seven parts on ITV.
Whereat this prodygal son of his tyme
Turned his unrestynge hande to pantomime:
Roome Atte The Botom Meets Dick Whittington
(Wyth Tomie Steele and Twiggie) was put on
Atte the Palladium. It ranne and ranne!

Was there no stoppynge thisse creative manne?
Alas! His ice showe flop't. His Muse, for once,
Now founde her litel lyre reft of stunts.
And now, with tenne yeeres gone, the noveliste
Muste needes revyve. And his psychiatriste
Together wyth his agente and, of course,
His thirde wife, feel a visyte to the source
Of his firste inspiration mighte wel loose
His writer's block; and—who can tel?—produce
Downe Atte The Botom, or some other sequel
Whose spynne-off possibilities mighte equal
The pickynges of the firste. So here todaye
He goes in serche of Ernest Hemingwaye
(Whose nice short werdes our man always admir'd:
The hand, with polysyllables, growes tired);
He trekkes to Paris, thence to Rome, and soon
Will lie beneeth Pamplona's risynge moon
And fille his dreggy cuppe at thatte fresshe spring
Where Papa roared, biside the bloodstayned ring.
But things are not quyte alwayes as they seem—
Hee has wyth him an Outsyde Broadcast teeme.

Acrosse the aisle, two HIPPIES sat entwyned,
Hopynge, ere longe, to blowe their tiny minde
Upon the Golden Roade to Samarkand,
Then on across the Kush, through Kashmir, and
At last drop out in distant Khatmandu,
Where grass is not just greene, but cheeper, too.
And there, atte some sleeke Maharishi's foote,
They wil spil oute the necessarye loote
To buy such solace as the saint may proffer
Wythinne the termes of Thysse Month's Special Offer.
I fynde I greeve for thysse unhappie lotte
Whose yung lyves runne increasingly to potte;
Who shal we blayme if, spaced out, zonked, they roame,
Seekynge some mysticke cobblers far from home?
Since we, all shackled in our bourgeois harness,
Can only crie: Yes, we have no Nirvanas!

Behynde these satte another lovynge paire,

Thir fingers loste in one another's haire;
A fond GAY COUPLE, bounde for Old Tangier
(A pilgrimage they mayke yeere after yeere).
These worshyppe atte the shryne of Oscar Wilde,
And André Gide, thatte othere faerie's childe,
Whose fin-de-siècle wand'rings inne the soukhs
(So taystefullie recycled inne his bokes)
Soon gayve Moroccan tourism a booste
Stil undiminished; for they have produced
(I feere I rayse uponne the reeder's neck a
Hackle) a kind of homosexual Mecca;
Where all the flockyng hordes of gay devoute
May—in the jargonne of thir faythe—come oute.
I wysshe them wel: for *chacun à son goût*,
And who am I, or (wyth respeckte) are you
To say that lit'ry pilgryms shal conforme
To sum olde-fashioned arbitrarie norm?
That onlie those who trek to Brontë doors
Shal be allowed enjoymente on the Moors?

Another wyth us wold not see this waye:
He stoode and stared atte them; he was not gaye
Inne any sense: al pinstryped stoode he there,
And close-cropped, groomed and gleemynge, was his hayre.
His firme grippe held a newe attaché-case,
Sharp-edged, with snaplockes (not unlyke his face).
A BUSINESSMANNE was he, and that an able,
Reared, thoroughbredde, in some goode British stable:
Eton, the Guards, perhaps an LL. B.,
Or else (from Oxenforde) a Greats degree.
At all eventes, a manne wyth Greeke and Latyn,
As polished as the leather chayre he satte in
At Knatchbull, Breene & Smythe (Precision Tools),
His father's firme. He wold not suffer fooles
Gladlie or otherwyse: a chappe who coulde
Not shoote, hunte, fishe or choose the proper woode
Or iron, or thoughte thatte footeball was a gayme
Played with a rounde ball, did not fynde his name
Among the list of clients at KBS.
Wich may explayne the roten bluddy mess

54

The companye was inne; and why this wighte
Was waytinge for a (cheep excursion) flyte
To Boston, and the Harvarde Bisnesse Schoole
In wich this upryte, dapper, sportynge foole
Had been thatte weeke (agaynste his wil) enrolled
By al his borde. For they had herde it tolde
Thatte at this founte of holy bisnesse writ
A sowe's eer mighte be processed and made fit
To be a purse, and thenne investment cashe
Would beate a path and begge the righte to stashe
Itself therein. And κBS wold rise,
A pheenix, to amayze the doubtynge eyes!
It maye be so: myself, I cannot feel
Much hope of succour to the bisnesse weal;
I saw his luggage: rods, a rydinge hatte,
Four tennys racquettes and a cricket batte.

Not far from him, a small, svelte figure satte,
Be-cloked, carnationed, in an opera hatte;
(He wore his opera hatte one day a weeke,
One day his anti-Russian one, and eek
A thirde, reserved for twittynge Wedgwood Benn.)
A MUSIC BUFFE (and Conscience For All Men),
Now bounde for Bayreuth and some Wagnerfest,
That shryne he worship't above al the reste
(Thrilled by the thought that it was Wagner, who
Wold happilie have turned him into glue?)
'Surely you're Bernard Levin, sir!' I cryed;
He turned, he smiled, he hummed awhile, he sighed,
And then began a sentence. But, alas!
Hardlie ten minutes were allowed to pass
Bifor they called Flyte BE 151,
And stil his sentence was not half-waye done.
(Wich onlie shows how German influence
Wil sometymes lead to compromise with sense;
How, with my aircraft throbbynge atte the kerbe,
Could I hang onne for Mister Levin's verb?)

Thus, on a suddenne, was I called awaye,
Torne from my felaweship, the straighte, the gaye,

The godlie and the mammonite, the freake,
And al the reste I have no tyme to speke
Of. All those goodlie soules, I feere, remayne,
Stil earthbounde, meeklie waytinge for thir playne.
While you, deere reeder, for thir grippynge tales,
Muste needes hange on, and trimme your eeger sayles
Until such tyme as they returne once more
To shayre the riches of thir blessèd store.
I have no doubte, though, that thir diff'rent tripps
Wil much improve what falls from al thir lipps,
Wen, havynge trod their spiritual paths,
They laye the fruits bifor us: how the baths
In Bethlehem were filthy, how the flies
Were everywhere in Lourdes, and what grate lyes
The brochures tolde! And how the bluddy guides
Robbed Martha blind! We'll heare it all, wyth slides.

Spires, What Are Ye Dreaming Now?

Oxford University's announcement that it faces a deficit of almost half a million in the next financial year and that it is entertaining a number of schemes to raise and save money, moved me beyond words, almost.

'HE DOAN PLANT TATERS,' sang the navvies, 'he doan pick cotton . . .'

Beneath their picks and pulverisers, the Motorway nibbled millimetrically on. Through the haze rising from the air-compressor, the Radcliffe Dome shimmered in the far distance, and beyond the bulldozer's cowling, Magdalen College tower poked up like a second exhaust spout.

'An' them as plants 'em is soon for . . .'

Suddenly, the roar and the clatter and the singing died on an instant, simultaneous.

'Whistle's went!' cried the foreman, and the gang fell out. They lay on what would one day be the hard shoulder, and gnawed at rolls, and pulled their knotted handkerchiefs off and wiped their sodden necks.

'It is not often appreciated,' said the Professor of Medieval Music, picking a curl of clay from his sledge, 'that Dowland owes remarkably little to Andreas Vogelsang's *Musicae Activae Micrologus*.'

'Begob,' said his mate.

'Quite,' said the Professor of Medieval Music. 'Of course, Dowland is not exactly my period, but I have always flirted with the later lute.'

'And why not?' said his mate. 'Ye're a long time dead.'

'I cannot, however,' said the Professor of Medieval Music, 'stand the sound of the lutina.'

'Dat bogger,' said his mate.

Oxford were eight lengths up as they shot Barnes Bridges, and forty-two seconds inside the record. Like an octopod water-boatman, the shell skimmed the bright surface, hardly, it seemed, touching the water at all. And then, at the very second that the cox emerged from the brickwork's shadow, his mega-phone swung upwards towards the craning cameras and bel-lowed:

'IT'S WHAT . . .'

'. . . . YOUR RIGHT ARM'S FOR!' screamed the eight, in perfect (as always) unison.

And held aloft their eight monogrammed tankards.

The producer leaned over the parapet.

'Sorry, everyone!' he cried. 'Could we take it from the top again, with just a teensy bit more wow?'

In the distance, Cambridge dwindled to a heaving dot.

In the North Schools lecture hall, motes eddied in the sun-beams. The atmosphere was taut, the hum of the packed audi-ence near-hysterical. Not a chair was vacant, which was remarkable, given that the cheapest seat was £1.50; and those who could not sit packed every aisle and niche.

There were, of course, few undergraduates present at that price. The thousand or so spectators were mainly American and Japanese tourists, the more sporting element among the Oxford townspeople, and those ladies with time on their hands who will always foregather at the chance to exchange folding money for the sight of blood.

At three p.m., precisely, to a fanfare by the popular All Souls Banjo Band, the two contestants stepped into the ring and shuffled in the mandatory resin. Still in their woolly dress-ing-gowns, they flexed themselves on the ropes, sucked on their gumshields, sparred against the cornerposts, nodded, at last, their readiness.

'INNA RED CORNAH,' cried the Warden of Wadham, 'AT ONE HUNNERDANFORTY POUNDS, THE REGIUS PROFESSOR OF MODERN HISTORY, THE AUTHAH OF THE LAST DAYS OF HITLAH, THE RISE OF CHRISTIAN EUROPE, AND THE REFORMATION AND SOCIAL CHANGE,

EDITAH OF THE POEMS OF RICHARD COBBETT—HUGH REDWALD
TREVOR-ROPAH!'

The Regius Professor bobbed to the centre of the ring, ac-
knowledging the echoing cheers.

'AND INNAH BLUE CORNAH,' screamed the MC, 'AT ONE HUN-
NERD-ANTWENNYTWO POUNDS, A FELLOW OF MAGDALEN COLLEGE,
A FELLOW OF THE BRITISH ASSOCIATION, AUTHAH OF THE ORIGINS
OF THE SECOND WORLD WAR, EDITAH OF THE DIARY OF THE
FAMOUS DAVID LLOYD GEORGE, RENOWNED SUNDAY EXPRESS
PHILOSOPHER—ALAN JOHN PERCIVALE TAYLAH!'

'I want a good clean fight,' said the Master of Balliol, 'break
when I say break, in the event of a knockdown go to a neutral
corner, now shake hands and come out fighting!'

The two contestants padded back to their seconds and
waited, panting slightly, for the bell.

'Pass the decanter,' murmured the Dean of New College.

The Jacobean crystal glinted as it swung, striking mellow
sparks from the Georgian silver that lay upon the dark Elizabe-
than oak. The Dean of New College held the warm liquor to the
light, and sniffed at it, and rolled it around his practised palate,
and let it slide down his throat. He closed his eyes, and thought
awhile.

'Not', he said, at last, 'a great Wincarnis. But a good Wincarnis.'

'Jesus, Howard, it has real, you know, mullions!' cried Mrs
H. B. Finemesser III, of Bismarck, N. Dakota. She turned to the
cringing figure in the creased white coat. 'How old is it, porter?'

'Brasenose College was founded in 1509, madame. This is
one of our oldest rooms. Also one of our best.'

'For forty dollars a night,' muttered H. B. Finemesser III,
squirting an aerosol at the mattress, 'it ought to be.'

'That tree outside the window, sir, was planted before
Columbus discovered . . .'

'It looks like they plumbed the goddam bidet in the same
day,' snarled the head of Finemesser Analine Substitutes.

'Ha, ha, ha, sir, very good, sir, I can see you have a wonderful
sense of humour, sir, I'll be, er, leaving you now, sir, ahem!'

'We'll breakfast at nine sharp,' said H. B. Finemesser III.

'Yes sir, of course, sir, well, I'd better be going, sir, is there anything else, sir, ahem, ahem?'

H. B. Finemesser poked about in the unfamiliar coinage, and plucked out a florin.

'God bless you, sir,' said the Senior Tutor of BNC, tugging his residual forelock and backing gratefully out.

On the top floor of the ivy-clad Gothic folly that towered beside the Woodstock Road, Zuleika crossed her lovely legs and smiled uncertainly at the fresh-faced undergraduate blushing on his knees beside her.

'Oh, Rodney!' she breathed, 'I'm terribly, terribly flattered, of course, but . . .'

'You would make me,' cried the undergraduate, 'not merely the happiest chap in all Oxford, Zuleika, but the happiest chap in all England! Please say yes, my darling!'

Zuleika looked away, and her eyelashes swept long cool shadows down her lovely cheeks, and she shook her golden head.

'I've thought about it, Rodney,' she murmured. 'Do not for a moment think that I haven't. But it is a frightfully, frightfully important decision for a gel, and I do not feel I am ready to take that enormous step.'

Rodney Puse-Belfiggling rose suddenly to his feet, and at his cry the swallows nestling in the dark eaves beyond the casement fled in twittering alarm.

'Very well then, Zuleika!' he exclaimed. 'I had not wished to play my trump card, but destiny leaves me no option! Remember that I am Captain of Boats, Rugger, Cricket, and Five Card Stud! If you will not do it for me, then, since I shall have no other course but to leave the University forthwith, do it for Oxford!'

'For Oxford!' gasped the delectable vision. She clasped her hands. 'Very well, then, Rodney, for Oxford!'

'Huzzah!' cried Rodney, and strode to the door. 'I'll send the first one up, my dearest!'

Zuleika removed her lovely hat.

'I must say, Rodders, a fiver a time doesn't sound very much.'

'Plus a quid for the maid, remember,' said Rodney.

Partridge in Pear Tree for Sale, makes Wonderful Chips

McGraw-Edison Company,
Parkade Plaza,
Columbia,
Missouri 65201.   29 December 1974

DEAR SIR:
I enclose, in case you have forgotten it, your recent advertisement in the *New Yorker* in which you offered an item for, and I quote, 'those who appreciate the finest in art and toasters'.

As a person of this kind, I was delighted to receive this opportunity of a lifetime on Christmas Day from my dear wife, Alice, formerly Miss Alice Terwilliken of Gazebo, Maryland, where her family have earned the respect of all for nearly three generations. I say this only to point out that my wife is also a person of the type you specify, having helped organise the Gazebo Museum of Maryland Art, with its many fine jugs and samplers, and also visited, with me, the Louvre of Paris and seen the Mona Venus in all its very old splendour during the recent Europe convention of top chromium executives of which I am one of, and proud to represent not only my company but also these United States, at Rome, Italy.

As you say in your ad, your Springbok Toaster came with its own serial number and certificate of authenticity, for which I was very grateful, as there is nothing worse than owning a fake pop-up toaster and work of art combined; we have a wonderful home full of valuable Louis XIX furniture purchased on our trip, including the chair Marie Antoinette was sitting on when they cut her head off, and it would be tragic to louse it up with a toaster where people came in and said 'That's a phony, don't you people know a bum artwork when you see one?'

**TOASTMASTER OFFERS YOU FINE ART THAT ALSO MAKES BREAKFAST.
THE LIMITED-EDITION SPRINGBOK TOASTER.**

The Springbok is for those who appreciate the finest in art and toasters.
It's a one-of-a-kind interpretation of an original painting by a well known American
wildlife artist. This work of art captures the elegant beauty of the Springbok Gazelle
in all its natural warm earthtones. In turn, Toastmaster was able to faithfully
reproduce the subtle coloration on long-lasting porcelain enamel panels that have
a matte finish to give the look and feel of the original canvas.
Certainly, it's the only fine art piece in the world that can prepare all kinds
of toaster foods. And prepare them well,

Also, we were both very impressed with the quality, and my wife joins me in saying where it beats her how you can do it for only $29.95. You say that 'Toastmaster was able to faithfully reproduce the subtle coloration on long-lasting porcelain enamel panels that have a matte finish to give the look and feel of the original canvas', and you are absolutely right! Many of our friends who we asked over to feel our toaster expressed amazement that, if you shut your eyes, you would think you were feeling an old master. One close friend, and he really knows about these things being a member of the Print Of The Month Club and someone who regularly goes out of his way to see a black-and-white movie, said that the last time he felt anything that good, it was a Rembrandt.

You say 'It may be a collector's item someday', and my wife and myself readily concur in this, since we already have a collection of pop-up toasters of which this will certainly be the showpiece. We did not collect these with an artistic view in mind, since none of them contains a genuine signed picture on it, let alone has the look and feel of canvas; no, we collected them because in most cases they only popped up for around a week or so, then they started to burn the toast black and crumble it and throw it around the room and all that kind of stuff which, as you know, is what toasters do after a while.

It is that which brings me to the, like, nub of my enquiry today. In your advertisement, as you can see, you say 'Certainly, it's the only fine art piece in the world that can prepare all kinds of toaster foods', and this is that to which I am taking exception to, on account of it doesn't, and this gives me something of a problem.

I am very partial to Welsh rabbit. This is not, of course, an animal of any kind, being a toasted item, and speaking as one who is fond of all of God's creatures (which is another reason for my delight at having a genuine Springbok Gazelle on the side of my toaster), I am not the kind of a man who would stick a rabbit in a toaster, even if you could force it into the slot, which I personally doubt, without bending or otherwise damaging the valuable work of art. No, Welsh rabbit is toasted cheese-on-toast, and as such comes under the heading, I would have thought, of 'all kinds of toaster foods'. At least, I would have thought it until quite recently, i.e. last evening, when my dear wife had to go out, as usual, to her evening course on The Negro Past And Present which is helping her to, you know, understand things besides just art etcetera. Anyway, she asked should she fix me something, and I said: 'No, dear, I will fix myself something on my wonderful Christmas gift, that way I can eat and improve my mind at the same time'.

So I put a nice thick slice of Swiss cheese on a slice of bread and butter, and I put it in my new toaster, and I pushed down the slide, and it came on perfectly, and I sat back to gaze at my limited edition, marvelling at the look of original canvas and thanking the Lord that I lived in a country where, despite panics over world inflation and oil and so forth, a connoisseur could still pick up a masterpiece at only $29.95. It was while I was pondering these things that I became aware of an extremely unsavoury smell which seemed to be issuing from my work of art. Even as I wondered about this, there was a big flash, and a plume of smoke came out of the slot, right about where the Springbok Gazelle's head is located.

I turned off the switch and examined my gift.

It transpires that I now have a work of art with cheese in its mechanism. I am afraid, too, that in the panic that followed this untoward downturn in my, or rather, my wife's investment, I hid the damaged item and opened the windows to clear the smoke etcetera. Luckily, my wife came in late—she had stayed behind to ask a question about sweat glands—and did not enter the kitchen before retiring. And this morning, I made a point of coming downstairs early to prepare breakfast so that I could make the family's toast in one of our old toasters, which was not the spiritual and educational experience I have become used to since Christmas Day, but at least it turned the goddam bread brown.

So my wife still does not know of the incident, and here I am at my office seeking your expert guidance. I guess I could have this toaster repaired, but I know that the restoration of a work of art is a delicate and expert technique, and I do not want some ordinary electrician lousing up my limited edition. Even if I send it back to you and the original artist, I have my doubts: will it still count as an original work of art even if it has new works? It seems to me it will be a reproduction, and that the accompanying certificate of authenticity will therefore be worthless. Should I forget about it as a working toaster altogether, and hang it on the wall as just a work of art? I have thought of this, but it occurs to me that part of its value comes from the fantastic way it combines art and toast, and if it can only do one thing, i.e. be art, then it is not much good, added to which a toaster is damned difficult to hang, being much wider than a painting, and people will bang their heads walking past. This will give rise to embarrassing situations, such as your guest dabbing his forehead and saying 'What the hell *is* that and why is it hanging there?' and you explain that it is a work of art and toaster combined, and he says 'Then why isn't it standing on a table where it can toast?' and you explain that it has cheese in it and does not work, and he says 'Then what do you mean it is a work of art and toaster combined, if it doesn't damn well toast?'

Personally, I like a good conversation about aesthetics, but I do not want one every time a friend opens his head up on my Springbok Gazelle.

Do you think I ought to buy another? My worry about this is that the more original art works of this kind there are in circulation, the less each one will be worth, and, anyway, what do I do with the busted one?

I mean, people like me, it goes against every principle we

have to throw a work of art in the trashcan, also if word gets around or someone sees it in my garbage, it could knock the bottom out of the whole market.

Please advise me soonest. I know you have a deep appreciation of artistic things, and I look to you for help in my hour of need.

Yours truly,
Edgar J. Milbro

It Can't Happen Here
(For a Week or Two, Anyway)

Now that Chile's military dictatorship has joined the growing list of juntas currently controlling large chunks of this planet, what chances are there that Britain's spreading disillusionment with conventional politics will one day be met with a nationwide broadcast like this?

GOOD EVENING, BRITAIN!

As of 08.00 this morning, the government of these islands has been placed in the hands of a democratically elected, twelve-man, military junta. I can personally vouch for that election, because I was there, and we all put our names in the hat, and when we looked in it, they were still there, and so we took them out again, and as senior officer present, it fell to my happy lot to become your Prime Minister.

It was, of course, no ordinary hat, but a tin one; a fact that will not, I appreciate, register with the long-haired, reefer-smoking poofters for which the silent majority of this great nation once fought in hats like these (*puts on hat*) and were proud, nay, conscripted, to do so. The dent (*indicates dent with left index digit*) was, you will be interested to learn, inflicted upon this British hat by a Hun, or as we used to call them, Boche, a few years prior to our grovelling and snivelling entry into the so-called Common Market; where we have, until this afternoon, had to conjoin our lot with those same Wop hordes who once ran shrieking from our Sheffield bayonets across British Egypt, and the garlic-reeking, sex-mad French who, you will recall, preferred to sit on their bums and watch the BEF pushed into the sea rather than face Adolf Hitler, the father of modern Germany.

Ours was no easy choice. We in the British Army have quite enough to do without going about being Home Secretary and Minister of Transport and so forth. Like so many others, I joined for the unrivalled water-ski-ing opportunities, and there will be precious little of that in Whitehall in the stern days ahead, I can tell you. Nevertheless, we have responded to the call of duty, and all that that entails, in preference to continuing under the yoke of crazed civilian organists in the pay of union Bolshies. Ah, I hear you cry, there are alternatives! Yes, I reply, and would you be happy beneath the rule of either a male Gracie Fields whose every action induces his troops to further mutiny, or a fop known mainly for his impressions of Charles de Gaulle?

Britain is ripe for a new sort of Government: reports have shown (*waves piece of paper*) that the British people are sick and tired of subsidising abortion with overpriced beef and paying surtax so that hospital beds may be provided for layabouts who would rather keep the Chinese opium trade in business with generous dole money than do a fair day's work for a fair day's pay. Well, Mr Mao Tse-tung, today's the day we spoil your little game! You may hug the loathesome Giscard to your yellow bosom, you may bring your abominable tin horses to these shores, but this so-called detente cuts no ice with men whose grandfathers were in Shanghai with Chinese Gordon and can fairly claim to know the Oriental mind backwards; which is, of course, the way it works.

What then, I hear you ask, are your Government's priorities? Let me answer that by asking the projectionist to put up the first slide:

Those of you familiar with modern television will, of course, recognise what that was: pornography. You can tell it's pornography by the lascivious smile and those two huge things attached to the front of the woman. Well, that's the last time you see any of that kind of filthy muck in the home. We in the Armed Forces know more about pornography than all your sex-crazed, Kremlin-subsidised, probably Levantine, trendy sociologists put together, and I think I speak for all senior officers who have ever looked at a red-eyed, white-faced regiment on the morning after an ENSA show and wondered how on earth we're ever going to get them to die with some measure of dignity. Indeed, most military experts agree that the Italian obsession with big thingummies and the nameless practices of Huns in the occupied countries were in no small measure responsible for the defeat of the Axis. What the Japs got up to, God only knows, but if some of today's bearded leftist swine had seen some of the Oriental sex-books it has been my misfortune to collect over the years, there'd be a lot less mealy-mouthed claptrap spouted about Hiroshima, you can be sure of that! Your Government's first priority, therefore, is to stop the peddling of

68

filth which is rotting men's minds and undermining production.

If any member of the public finds himself having difficulties in this area, he is advised to contact his MP, who will be only too glad to lay on some water-ski-ing.

Pornography brings me, naturally enough, to health and the social services, and let me say at the outset that your Government has every intention of maintaining a public welfare system *where it is deserved*. However, your Government is no stranger to the practice of malingering, and when I tell you that the Minister of Social Services once captured a Boche machine-gun post despite the loss of his left arm, right leg, and both ears, you will appreciate that short shrift will be given to trouble-making Red layabouts attempting to sabotage the national effort by using broken legs as an excuse for latecoming. As this slide shows:

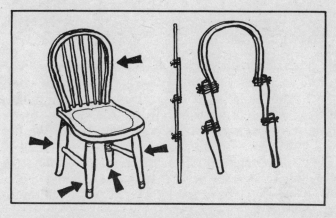

any kitchen chair may be used to furnish up to three splints and two crutches, and at a fraction of the usual cost. Leaflets on tourniquets, morning sickness, home dentistry, silicosis, and simple brain surgery will be available from your local Department of Social Security, free of charge.

We hear a lot today about something called economics; well, when I was a boy, the word for it was hard work, and a lot of namby-pamby bleating about balance of payments crises or trade deficits and suchlike panics brought on by a load of foreigners, non-combatant Swiss usurers, and the general riffraff of Europe will not wash with me or the rest of my chaps. We have a straightforward approach to all these so-called problems, best summed up, I feel, in this simple diagram:

As you can see, with the aid of six long poles and an adequate amount of stout rope, it is possible to overcome virtually every obstacle this country is likely to meet in the foreseeable future. If the going does get rough, of course, we can always declare war, which, as every cadet knows, is merely the continuation of politics by other means. Personally, I am of the firm opinion, in which I am not alone in Whitehall, that Zurich could be taken and held by a single division; and as to the threat of the German mark, your Chancellor of the Exchequer has already come to me this afternoon and informed me that he is only too ready to take another crack at the swine, preferably from the South.

This brings me to foreign policy. I think many of you will recognise this shape,

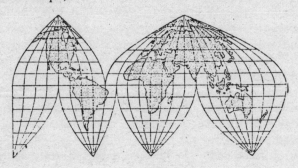

though not, sadly, its colour. I myself have been so heavily engrossed over the past few years in my major study *Mind-Rotting Filth And Its Effect Upon Victorian Cavalry Tactics* that I had not noticed, until taking office this morning, that the Empire as I remember it has almost entirely disappeared, taking with it innumerable opportunities for water-ski-ing. Much of Africa seems to be called something else, and when I discovered that the care of India had been given into the hands of a native woman of some kind, I there and then determined upon a course of action which will not be completed until our cannon stand once more at the gates of Rangoon.

Where, you enquire, shall we find the men, where the money? It so happens that earlier in the afternoon, my Minister of Education came to me, greatly distressed, to inform me that something like four hundred thousand young men are currently engaged in what is laughingly termed further education, and that the British taxpayer has been supporting these shaggy-locked, pimple-infested, free-loving anarchists with hundreds of millions of pounds which have been squandered on Communist literature, posters of South American terrorist gang-leaders, and birth control devices the sophistication of which leaves the decent Englishman agog! Had we had funds of this sort in May 8, 1945, we could have hitched up our belts, taken five for a smoke, and pushed the Stalinist scum back to the Volga, as Winston wished.

It is not too late.

I see an education policy, staggering in its vision, unbounded in its promise, in which the august halls of learning in this great country are finally purged of the lust-broken, trouble-making intelligentsia and filled with a whole new race of students buckling down to the discipline of wireless telegraphy, gun-laying, tank maintenance, field cookery, dressage, shooting, marching, gassing, with, of course, ample time for water-ski-ing, lotto, and an informal monthly dance to English tunes with a recognisable melody.

My fellow-Englishmen, this is a great night for our country! I know how many of you have grown sick and tired of the mealy-mouthings of previous tenants of this proud address, of the men who have promised that England shall be a haven for the fuzzy-wuzzy, a paradise for the pornographers, an open cheque for the abortionist and pimp and swarthy usurer. I promise you only glory and a return to those great days of our common heritage that gave us Passchendaele and the Somme, to the firm purpose that put us in the forefront of contemporary hanging, to the resolve that took Africa away from the unenlightened hottentot and put it in Threadneedle Street where it belonged, to a concept of home and family which ensured that the merest child could play his own part in the national effort with his own little pick and shovel, to an idea of Britain, in short, which will enable us to hold up our heads among the nations, always remembering, of course, to keep the chinstraps slack to reduce the risk of blast-decapitation, turn the eyes away from the flash, and leave all notes to next-of-kin in care of the Bereavements Officer, GHQ.

Thank you, and good night.

Will Dirty Old Men get a Fair Crack of the Whip?

AT FIRST I THOUGHT, NO. This cannot be. I have merely misread the item, that's all. That's what comes, I said to myself, of trying to read the *Daily Telegraph* by candlelight; an activity which, despite its curious appropriateness to that newspaper's general atmosphere, wrinkles the retina and throws strange shadows in the brain.

So I held the candle closer, ignoring the hiss of molten wax on cat. The animal, which had been huddling uncharacteristically against my lower limbs in the hope of gleaning a soupçon of shinny warmth in these powerless times, leapt up and ran shrieking from the room; which puzzled me for a moment. But only for a moment, for in the next all was made clear: it, like me, had also noticed the *Telegraph* story, and taken the only possible action. For some time thereafter, man and cat ran about the darkened house, shrieking, victims both of the world's weirdness, hands stretched across the great animal spectrum in mutual disbelief. Power cuts have their virtues, too.

'Dirty old men,' ran the item, 'are incapable of being corrupted any further, and as long as they make up the majority of regular customers a bookseller does not break the law in selling dirty books to them, two High Court judges decided yesterday.'

Below which mould-breaking decision hung a cautionary tale concerning policemen who had dared to run in a couple of decent citizens whom they had discovered selling *A History Of Knickers*, or some such, to Southampton's itinerant depraved. And short shrift the coppers got! It was a great moment, cheered, I'm sure, by hundreds of Dirty Old Men flocking the public gallery and waving their raincoats, if nothing more, in celebration of the new era.

The rights of the Dirty Old Man have been recognised in

73

law! A precedent has been created! Dirty Old Manpower has hurled its underprivileged members onto the statute books as citizens in good standing, if that's the expression I'm after. The High Court, in that infinite wisdom that only age can bring, has finally removed the terrible social stigma that has for so long so unfairly attached to elderly gentlemen who wander about allotments in the gloaming, dispensing a peppermint here, a friendly pat there, a smile for everyone. For, by refusing to penalise the sturdy bookseller who supplies their demand, by keeping him open to selflessly serve the needs of Southampton's geriatric swingers, what have their Honours done if not recognise the entitlement of yet another scourged minority to fair dos?

Of course, the recognition in law that total corruption is its own exoneration will, with luck, touch everybody. Indeed, touching everybody will itself soon be established as man's inalienable right, I'll be bound. Or, at least, you'll be bound: personally, my taste does not run to thong and reef-knot, but no matter, in the bright new millennium there'll be something for all, and those of us whose fancy runs to standing in a bath of tepid Bovril while acolytes smite us with old wellies shall want for nothing. For this enlightened judgment does not affect merely today's sprightly OAP, it lays down a pattern over which generations yet unwithered will rejoice and coo.

For we shall all be DOMs, one day. With luck, that is, since whoever heard of a Clean Old Man? One is either a DOM or dead. That is the way it is (as Hemingway wrote so penetratingly in his magnificent *The Dirty Old Man And The Sea*, a tale of offshore smut that has lain too long neglected and will now, doubtless, soon see the light. Or, at least, the half-light). How reassuring it is to know that when we have passed the age of consent on the far side, we shall not be forced to creep like criminals from door to door, begging for favours! How unglamorous to be known as a Dirty Old Man, but how thrilling to bear the title Totally Corrupt! Shades of Baron Charlus and Adolphe Menjou! Echoes of the grand days in Le Touquet when no boulevardier worth his salt, let alone his oats, would stroll into the salons de jeu before his sixtieth birthday, a pearl stick-pin in his cravat, a gold topped cane in his hand, and a pellet of monkey gland under his tongue, his grey kid glove flitting from knee to knee and bum to bum with all the zesty agility of a pubescent bat!

Of course, thoughts of monkey gland and such inevitably call to mind the distasteful side of the whole subject: commercialism. But business is business, and the world of commerce exists to satisfy those needs which society recognises and, as now, endorses. One just hopes that DOMs will not be exploited, that's all; that the decent pornographer who has slaved for this day so hard and so long will not see his pioneering capitalised upon by fly-by-night operators eager to cash in on the DOM boom, unprincipled men who will not hesitate to corner the market in Ordnance Survey maps of Hampstead Heath and Streatham Common and flog them at inflated prices to the newly-liberated hordes of excited oldies flocking to London's greensward in their shuffling thousands. One prays that nasty Dirtythèques will not suddenly mushroom all across the realm, charging a quid a time for watered lime-juice to DOAPs lured in by neon suspender and Dayglo clog. Blue movies, naturally, will flourish unraided, provided no one is admitted under the age of seventy (or sixty-five, accompanied by their fathers); and may well, as their establishments proliferate and go legit, bang up their admission prices in the crazed demand.

But there may be even less desirable side-effects, spawned by greed: a run on boiled sweets, say, bringing an infant backlash in its wake, an escalation in sou'wester costs, leaving the lifeboatmen to rattle their collection boxes in vain, a thinning of soccer crowds and bowling-club support as oldies seek participation sports instead, and a commensurate rise in rush hour chaos as the tubes fill with cheery frotteurs, riding the rails all day for a 5p ticket, warm, snug, and endlessly a-grope, pointing out to railway police forcing through the packed carriages of trains wrenched to a halt by frantic communication cords that the law cannot touch them on the grounds that they're Totally Corrupt, and there's an end.

Doubtless the package-tourmongers will not be slow to leap upon this jumbo bandwagon: having already cut their winter losses with offers of fiver-a-time fortnights for oldies, what can stop the rise of Domtours and Smutways, promising cut-rate flights to watch nubile Spanish maids beat carpets beneath your own private Costa Bravan balcony? Be tucked up at night by lovely resident duennas who leave you to your Ovaltine and dreams; admire lush teenagers changing on the sands from the privacy of your own beach-hut knothole; have your shoulder brushed by an air-hostess's plump hip as you loll aboard our sunbound 707 (in-flite skinflix at nominal surcharge). Endless, endless, the profitable temptations!

Still, with all the waiting pitfalls, the man of sensitivity must still rejoice. We have a future now, we junior satyrs, we apprentice DOMs; more waits for us than the knitted woolly and the tartan slipper and the companionship of a mangy dog; our sensual future holds more than an annual colonic irrigation or a rare furtive nudge in a foggy bus queue. Retirement, men, is not the end. It is not even the beginning of the end. But it is, perhaps, the end of the beginning.

You should live so long.

Long Ago and Far Away

Much talk is talked of the need for the Dunkirk spirit today. But suppose instead that we had had today's spirit at Dunkirk?

UP TO HIS WAIST in the filthy sea, oil lapping his sodden webbing, bomb-blasted flotsam bobbing about him, he sucked his teeth, and shook his head.

'I'm not bleeding going in that,' he said, 'I'm not bleeding going home in no rowing boat.'

'Right,' said his mate.

'Eighteen blokes in it already,' he said. 'Conditions like that, they're not fit for a pig.'

'Not fit for a pig, conditions like that,' said his mate.

'Got brought here in a troopship, din't we?' he said. He cupped his hands towards the rowing boat, and the man leaning towards them over its stern, arm outstretched. 'GOT BROUGHT HERE IN A BLEEDING TROOPSHIP!' he shouted, 'Ten square feet of space per man!'

'Regulations,' said his mate, nodding. 'All laid down. Nothing about going back in no bloody rowing-boat. Get away with murder if you let 'em, some people.'

A Stuka shrieked suddenly overhead, levelled, veered up out of its dive, back into the flakky sky. Its bomb exploded, drenching the two men.

'Not even got a roof on,' he said. 'What happens if it starts coming down cats and dogs halfway across? You could catch pneumonia.'

'Get a chill on the liver,' said his mate.

'*And* there's seasickness. It's not as if I'm a sailor. I'm not saying it isn't all right for *sailors*, am I? All right for them, open bloody boat. I mean, it's their line, know what I mean? But I'm

77

a gunner. That's what I got took on as, that's what I am. If I'd wanted to be a sailor, I'd have got took on as a sailor.'

'I'm a cook,' said his mate. 'Cook, I said when they asked me up the recruiting. I didn't say bleeding admiral. I didn't say, I want to be a cook on account of I'm interested in the standing up to me waist in water, did I?'

'Course you didn't.'

An Me109 came low over the surface, strafing the scummy sea. A machine-gun bullet took his hat away.

'You'd have got more as an admiral, too,' he said. 'You get compensation, working in filthy conditions. I reckon they owe us special benefits. Nothing about all this in basic training, was there? Prone shooting and a bit of the old bayonet, dry conditions, two bob a day, all meals.'

'When was the last time you had a square meal?' asked his mate.

'I never thought of that!' He took a notepad from his saturated battle-blouse, licked his pencil, scribbled. 'I never thought of that at all. Three days ago, as a matter of fact. Bleeding Cambrai, if you can call two spoons of warm bully a square meal.'

'FOR GOD'S SAKE GET A MOVE ON!' cried the man in the stern.

The two privates waded awkwardly forward.

'Not so bloody fast, mate,' said the first. 'I require a few moments with the brothers here.'

The eighteen stared at him over the gunwales. Red fatigue rimmed their eyes, their bandages were thick with oil, their helmets were gone, leaving their hair to whiten with the salt.

'It has been brought to my attention by Brother Wisley here,' he said, 'that we are being expected to work in conditions unfit for a pig. Not only are we not being allowed to pursue our chosen trade, we have been dumped here in what can only be described as the sea, we have been required to leave our tools behind on the beach, we have not had a square meal for three days, and as for the statutory tea-break, I can't remember when. I won't even go into the overtime question.'

'We won't even go into the overtime question,' said his mate. 'But may I draw the meeting's attention to the fact that members of the Kings Own Yorkshire Light Infantry can be seen on our left climbing into a cabin cruiser?'

The eighteen turned, and looked.

'Bloody hell,' said a corporal.

'Well might you say bloody hell, brother!' said the first private. 'Course, I'm not saying our brothers in the KOYLI are not entitled to what they can get, and good luck, but the anomaly of the heretofore mentioned situation currently under review before the meeting by which we of the Royal Artillery. . . .'

'And the Catering Corps.'

'. . . and the Catering Corps, Brother Wisley, thank you, by which we of the Royal Artillery and the Catering Corps do not enjoy parity is one which threatens all we hold most dear.'

'RIGHT!' cried the man in the stern, 'Get in, or shut up, we haven't got all damned day, Jerry's throwing. . . .'

The private held up his hand.

'Just a minute, squire,' he said, 'just a minute. After frank and free discussions with my ad hoc executive here, we regret to inform you that deadlock has been reached in the negotiations, and unless you are prepared to furnish us with such basic requirements. . . .'

'I'm getting out anyway, brother,' said the corporal. He eased himself over the side. 'Come on, you lot, I have no intention of allowing my brothers on the floor to be manipulated by a cynical management and subjected to actual distress to serve the whim of the bosses.'

'Well said, brother!' cried the private.

The eighteen slid into the icy water.

The rowing boat came about, and sploshed off towards another queue. But a bomb, exploding between it and them, gave the private time to wade up to the head of the line, and the man on crutches leading it.

'I know these are difficult times, brothers,' announced the private, 'but let us not use that as an excuse to allow ourselves to be led like lambs to the slaughter. Solidarity is our watchword, brothers.'

The line hesitated.

'We could be, er, needed back home,' said the man at the front, 'couldn't we?'

The private stared at him bitterly.

'Oh, got a troublemaker, have we?' he said loudly. 'It's amazing, there's always one, isn't there?'

'Always bloody one,' said a voice down the line.

'Thank you, brother.' He poked a finger into the leader's chest. 'You'll get that crutch across your bonce in a minute, son,' he said. He spread his hands to take in the gradually assembling crowd of waterlogged soldiers. 'Got a man here believes all he reads in the newspapers! Got one of your *thinkers*! Doesn't know all this scaremongering is just put about by the gumment to screw the working man, doesn't realise that your *real* situation is all very nice, thank you, doesn't . . .' The private broke off as a couple of Heinkels came howling in from the dunes, their tracer slicing a red swathe through the crowd, drowning his words '. . . doesn't appreciate that gumment propaganda is being cunningly directed to militate public opinion on the side of nationalistic interests contrary to the welfare of the entire work force, does he?'

'I think we ought to vote on it,' said a fusilier who had been standing next to a man dismembered in the last strafe.

'Oh, yes, and I don't think!' snorted the private. 'You won't catch me out with no snap show of hands, brother, contrary to the democratic secret ballot as we know it. I should cocoa!'

The men shifted their feet uneasily. The private had articulated it all so clearly, and, after all, the men who had brought the little boats were, for the most part, men of a class they had long learned to mistrust. Nor did they wish to betray their mates, with whom they had come through no small adversity; and it could not be denied that it was at just such fraught moments as this that advantage could be taken of them, with their defences down, and the odds in favour of those who sought to control them.

And, after all, were things so bad that they should forget all else but short-term salvation? They were not yet dead, were they, which was rather more relevant than the emotionally-loaded evidence that others could be seen to be dying. They had, had they not, stuck it out on the beach up until then, why should they not continue to stick it out now?

Slowly, but with what certainly appeared to be determination, the entire waiting army turned, and began to wade back towards the littered dunes, and the devil they knew.

There were, of course, one or two who glanced over their shoulders in the direction of England; but, naturally, it was too far away for them to be able to discern anything, even had the darkness not, by then, been falling.

Lost Horizon

SPEAKING AS ONE whose dear wife Phoebe was done over rotten by a dago wine-waiter with a wall eye in the trapped lift of the El Miraculo Hotel, Benidorm, and has insisted on separate beds ever since, I think I speak for all of us who are today mourning the untimely demise of the cheap package holiday.

It is the end of an era, as Sir Winston Churchill might have put it, had he ever danced the hokey-cokey beneath the romantic Spanish moon, while the Latin night filled with the heady scent of real imported bangers hopping and sizzling on the Free Fiesta Barbecue; or clapped and whistled as the wonderful flamenco ensemble and its mobile discotheque played *Happy Birthday* to a short sweating lady from Arnos Grove, and lovely scrubbers Rosita y Dolores snapped their plastic castanets and flashed their wincyette knickers, the flickering barbecue flames winking off their brass teeth, in an interesting dance about bringing home the pilchards.

Yes, in all the arguments between the Benns and Heseltines, in all the business supplement analyses concerning the economic structure of tourism, in all the heartbreak stories of stranded holidaymakers, not a word seems to have been said about the huge and terrible void that has opened up in the lives of those countless millions of us who have grown accustomed to spending the happiest fortnights of our lives upon the fabled costas of Europe, for not more than $39\frac{1}{2}$ gns, incl. all luggage labels.

Is it only a dozen short years since the first planeload of package tourists took off from Gatwick, having been carried there by bus from Luton following the row at Heathrow the day before when it was discovered that they should never have left Manchester Ringway in the first place? I myself was not on that pioneer trip, sadly, but my brother knew a man who had been invalided out of it and has always been proud of his association with someone who had taken part in the first conga ever to have been performed at thirty thousand feet.

It was to be two years before I embarked upon my own first package holiday, but Time will never erase the fond memories I have of the happy laughter of children (I think there were fifty-seven of them, not counting the one who was flushed over Biscay) as, seat-hopping around the aircraft in a wonderful game of their own devising, they walked through my lunch, deftly batting my toupee into the luggage rack with one adroit swing of their new shrimpnet. Before the cheap Spanish holiday began, of course, only the privileged few could ever take their children abroad to get sunstroke.

The sun, the sun! Shall we ever forget our first fine careless rapture as those health-giving Mediterranean rays struck our blanched bodies, ripening them to human plums in a mere hour? On my first trip, to Torremolinos, I believe it was, or possibly Marbella—somewhere, anyway, with stucco skyscrapers and Red Barrel (I have experienced so much of Espana, as we travellers call it, that I tend to confusion, except where Majorca is concerned, on account of it being the only place with draught E)—I removed my shirt and rolled up my flannels to the knee, as had been my wont at Herne Bay for the previous five seasons, and had to spend the next two nights standing in a corner of our bedroom, unable to lie flat, or indeed roll my trousers down again. How glad I was that the unfinished El Superbo still lacked a roof! The cooling dew settling upon my scarlet shoulders was boon indeed, despite dear Phoebe's derision when she awoke with the dawn's first bulldozer to find me steaming.

That, of course, was another great bonus of the cut-price holiday: the unpredictability of it all, the thrill of walking out onto a balcony that wasn't there yet and falling five flights into an ornamental garden consisting of breeze blocks for next season's annexe; those chance re-routings when, imagining that you would be arriving in Barcelona at eleven pm, just time for a quick Mackeson at the bar before strolling down to the colourful local taverna for a sausage toad and Bournvita, you suddenly found yourself instead on a piece of waste ground outside Alicante at three in the morning watching your tour-leader rolling on the ground with the company's local representative while babes in arms shrieked for their four o'clock feed and an unseasonal typhoon blew your carrier bags of duty-free Rothmans into the nearby sea. Or, hugging yourself at the miracle of modern travel, experiencing the thrill of going to sleep in Gatwick and waking up, through expert overbooking, in Gatwick.

Until 1960, very few Englishmen had ever gone down with dysentery, and those the privileged few fortunate to have been at Gallipoli or Tobruk, say, or in Burma during the appropriate season. But suddenly, within a few short years, thanks to advanced techniques that made it possible to site a hotel on an infested swamp, gum the building together in three days, and ensure that its waste conduits ran through the kitchens before opening five yards out to sea from the glorious partially-golden beach, thousands of Englishmen and women, and their offspring, were able to see everything from gastro-enteritis to botulism in a whole new light, an experience it is virtually impossible to enjoy in Weston-super-Mare. I believe it was St. Teresa of Avila who had much to say about the moral significance of acute pain bravely borne, but I do not recall where she was staying at the time, and I can only say that without paiella I should not be the man I am today. Food poisoning has also given us much in common, and many a delightful evening have I spent with erstwhile fellow-holidaymakers going through our slides and comparing trots.

Dear, oh, dear, here I am going on about the travel and the sun and the food and all the other wonderful physical experiences, and never a word about the broadening of the mind! And me with one of the largest collection of plastic bull's ear ashtrays in the Home Counties, many of them with mottoes for golfers on, and a Don Quixote with a lightbulb in his willie, not to mention two genuine scale-model toreadors, one with fags in, the other with matches. Also six hundred beermats, each of them calling up special and individual memories, including The Pig & Whistle, Malaga, where my brother-in-law Dennis hit a Swede, The Green Man, Tossa del Mar, and The Wagon & Horses, Ibiza, where Phoebe said the pickled onions had mould on and our youngest, Gerard, got a dart in his head.

Nor has it altogether been a one-way traffic, and Spain herself must today be grieving for what has been and will not ever be again. Once, so I understand it, the coasts of Spain were nothing but unsightly stretches of fishing villages, the ludicrous wooden boats lying untidily about on the beaches, unprofitable trees everywhere, and not a *Daily Express* or a bottle of Double Diamond available between Irun and Gibraltar. Many Spaniards had never heard of typewriters, let alone had more English secretaries than most people have had hot dinners, and frozen peas were entirely unknown. Today, there are eighty-one thousand identical facades facing the Mediterranean, either in white or in beige, and getting on for six million low-flush suites, plus pedalos capable of carrying more people in a single day than were ferried throughout the D-Day landings.

As for the increased bullfight demand, turnover is so enormous that in at least half a dozen places I personally know of, matadors are using pigs, and even, following the mushrooming of ten thousand mini-golf courses throughout the Iberian peninsula, considering the use of dwarfs to fight chihuahuas with toothpicks, so restricted is the space now available for new bullrings.

For Phoebe and myself, however, we shall not personally see subsequent developments. Already frightened by the trend of collapsing operators, we have decided to holiday this year on our own Sussex coast, and I do not see the future as offering any alternative. The bitter's bloody awful, not a patch on your genuine Majorcan keg, the chips are as soggy as amputated fingers, the band hasn't played *Knees Up Mother Brown* once since we've been here, and as for the tea, I wouldn't wash socks in it.

I suppose they *try* hard enough, but there's no getting away from it, it just isn't Spain.

Brother, Can You Spare an Hour?

British businessmen, according to the London Evening Standard, are complaining that attempts to export to the United States are being hampered by the old-fashioned image of Britain created by TV programmes like Upstairs, Downstairs and The Forsyte Saga and 'giving the impression that Britain is steeped in the past and not a nation building computers and Concordes'. Well, why on earth didn't they say so before? After all, a word here and there . . .

(*Fade in,* INTERIOR, DAY, *the Bellamy servants' quarters*)
Edward: O my gawd, snakes alive, whatever next, Mrs. Bridges, what is this what we are a-eating of now?
Mrs. Bridges: You 'old your tongue, young Edward, oo-er, coo, that is as tasty a piece of braised high-protein, low-chlorestorol, bio-degradable recycled filet-mignon-flavoured soya-derivative as ever I clapped eyes on, and at one shillin' a pound, less than a twentieth the price of best topside!
Edward: Lawks-a-mercy, Mrs. Bridges, only a shillin' a pound! Why, bless me and lor' love a duck, that ain't no more than twelve American cents! I do 'ope as 'ow we are still able to meet our vast export commitments what must be a-floodin' in!
Mrs. Bridges: Don't you worry your noddle about that, young Edward, you scallywag, 'Er Majesty the Queen's wonderful Department o' Trade and Industry is now blessed with as efficient an international sales force o' fine young gennelmen as ever set finger to pocket calculator, ain't that so, Mr. 'Udson?
Hudson: Och, weel, the noo, it dinna behove the like o' us wee folk tay pass judgement on our fine bonny rulers, ye ken, Mrs. Bridges, but I do happen tay have it on guid authority that yon Uberhauptausgezeichnetkreditanstalt o' Zurich think our wee balance o' payments has nay looked more bricht!

Rose: 'Ere, Mister 'Udson, ain't that the top Swiss bank what you are a-speaking' of, gorblimey?

Hudson: Aye, Rose, monny a winny mak' a gru, heh, heh, heh! But be off aboot your business noo, Rose, was that wee hum no the signal that our bonny Mostyn-Foskett Wundawosher has just finished doing the dishes in half the time o' its nearest competitor, at a mere fraction o' the cost?

Rose: Cor, Mister 'Udson, meanin' no disrespect but you ain't arf got good bleeding ears, that 'um is the quietest in the world, what wouldn't the Japs give to get their little 'ands on the secret!

Mrs. Bridges: Cor, Rose, you're a proper caution, whatever next, har, har, har, but get along now, I just 'eard Master James's 'Arrier Jump Jet land on the potting-shed, 'e'll want 'is bed turned down.

Edward: Crikey, I sometimes think Master James only joined the Royal Air Force for the unequalled opportunity it provided to fly the world's most advanced vertical take-off aircraft!

Hudson: Och, young Edward, are ye no' forgetting aboot the miraculous Condor air-to-air missile he'll be having such a guid time firing, beyond doot the cheapest and most effective in the entire Western world, an' no waiting upon delivery?

Mrs. Bridges: Landsakes, Mr. 'Udson, 'ow you men goes on! A person might never know these 'ere weapons o' yourn 'as led to a 'ole range o' wonderful domestic spin-offs such as the non-stick non-ferrous non-toxic egg-spoon with tasteful 'and-crafted Union Jack coddlin'-knob!

Hudson: Ye've a braw point there, Mrs. Bridges, but was that no' the chic bing-bong o' our noo Cheerigong All-British door-chime, and will I no' be away to answer it?

(*Fade out. Fade in* INTERIOR, DAY, *the Bellamy living-room*)

Bellamy: What is it, Hudson? You know how I prefer not to be disturbed when I am submitting my company reports to the *Guinness Book of Records*, justly famed British best-seller.

Hudson: I do indeed, sir, but it is a Mr. Soames Forsyte accompanied by other members of his family.

Bellamy: Ah! Well, show them in, Hudson, show them in!

Hudson: Mr. Soames Forsyte!

Bellamy: My dear Soames, how very good to see you!

Soames F: Excuse my somewhat bizarre attire, Bellamy, I am just this very hour back from examining our revolutionary new process for extracting plutonium from sleet. Let me introduce my cousin, Yakimoto Forsyte.

Yakimoto F: Mistah Berramy, this are great honnah! Engrish businessmen of your caribre will be salvation of Japanese economy! This are reason we are shifting entiah production of Forsytesan Industries to Engrand, incruding revorutionary new Forsyte Cherry people's rimousine!

Bellamy: You do me too much credit, sir! My incredible marketing successes would have been impossible without the co-operation of the English work force, whose reliability and pride in their impeccable craftsmanship is a legend, the maintenance of which is understandably the TUC's first priority. But excuse me, Soames, I do not believe I have had the pleasure of meeting these other gentlemen?

Soames F: Forgive me, Bellamy, may I present Werner von Forsyte, Commendatore Luigi Forsyte, Ingemar Forsyte of Copenhagen, and, of course, our dear American cousin, Groucho Forsyte.

All: Delighted! Entzückt! An honour, etc., etc.

Bellamy: My dear Soames, the international ramifications of your remarkable family never cease to amaze me!

Soames F: Well, yes, Bellamy, one must I feel hand it to Old Jolyon for realising all those years ago that mere land and money were not enough! And, of course, for having the, dare I say foresight. . . .

All: Yuk, yuk, yuk! Vot vit! Hirarious! Etc., etc.

Soames F: . . . to comprehend that England was part of a wider manufacturing and trading world, that being little Englanders would get us nowhere, that a pooling of various national resources, initiatives and currencies would someday be essential to a vigorous international capitalism that would be proof against all commie incursions and corruptions, and for laying down, if you will, ha, ha, ha, pardon the expression, the foundations of Forsyte International on the Grand Tour undertaken in his youth!

Groucho F: Gimme a man like Jolyon Forsyte every time, and if you can't gimme a man like Jolyon Forsyte, I'll take a woman like Raquel Welch, and bring me an order of cole slaw on the side, no dill and easy on the mayonnaise!

Bellamy: Well said, sir, I think that calls for a drink! I trust no-one has any objection to a fifteen-year-old single-malt Scotch which we are still able to produce for the almost unbelievably low cost of less than one hundred dollars a case, and what an executive gift it makes, eh? Excuse me, I'll just ring for Hudson. . . .

(*Fade out. Fade in* INTERIOR, DAY, *the servants' quarters*)

Mrs. Bridges: Meaning no disrespect, Mr. 'Udson, but I do wish as 'ow you wouldn't tinkle them glasses so! All that racket, we'll never 'ear Concorde passin' over, an' I promised that young nephew o' mine I'd take a snap of it with my new two-pound Instaroid camera wot not only develops its own pitchers in five seconds flat, it also sticks 'em in its own album an' puts itself away in the drawer.

Hudson: Och, Mrs. Bridges, I do beg your pardon, the noo, I was so admiring the glint and sheen o' the wonderful Webb crystal and marvelling aboot how England manages to do it at the price, ye ken, that I got quite carried away!

Mrs. Bridges: Yes, well, talking of carryin' things away, Mr. 'Udson, you'd best be orf with them drinks, it's been forty-six seconds since Mr. Bellamy rung, and you know 'ow he is about punctuality, efficiency, hard work, service standards, quality control and client satisfaction, don't you?

Hudson: I ken it well, Mrs. Bridges, I ken it well! But ye didna need to blather on like that, ye ken—all ye had to say was Mr. Bellamy's an Englishman!

Mrs. Bridges: Lor' lumme, Mr. 'Udson, what *will* that silver tongue o' yours say next!

(*Fade out.* MUSIC. CREDITS. LIST OF PRODUCTS MENTIONED. ORDER FORMS.)

When Dinosaurs Walked the Earth
(World Copyright Reserved)

A thirty-man expedition has just left for a jungle-covered plateau in Venezuela in quest of prehistoric life. They will descend into a giant hole, at the bottom of which, say the scientists, life forms have not undergone the mutations of evolution. Unfortunately, at the top of the hole they have: which may explain some of the differences between Sir Arthur Conan Doyle's Lost World and mine.

I WILL NOT BORE THOSE whom this narrative may reach by an account of our luxurious voyage upon the Booth liner, save that I should wish to point out that the Booth Lines new Sail 'n' Sun Getaway Family Cruises are a snip at only £235 per head, including personalised rug and half bottle of wine with evening meal, plus use of telescope when passing dolphins, and that I should like to extend the heartfelt thanks of Professor Challenger and the rest of our team to Booth Lines for their generosity in transporting us to our destination, coupled with the name of Captain Enrico Gomez de Hoja, who will be among the first guests on my new TV chat show along with Henry the Pterodactyl, now happily under contract to one of our foremost birdseed advertisers.

We reached Caracas on the forenoon of the 18th, and encountered nothing more than the normal difficulties in disembarking our videotape and film equipment, our camera teams, our agents, managers, make-up ladies, publicity personnel, and endorsing representatives, although some inconvenience, it must be said, was caused by the Conservative politician who had joined our party as an independent factfinder and took the opportunity of delivering an impassioned speech on the Government's fiscal policy to a party of Carmelite nuns temporarily caught on the gangplank by their hems until he was thrown into the dock by a group of Brazilian longshoremen whipped to a frenzy by his Labour pair who had been denouncing Phase III through a megaphone on the poop.

These interruptions having been sorted out, the leaders of the party repaired to the sumptuous fazenda proffered us by the chairman of Jungle Jollidays Inc., Venezuela's most enterprising tour operator, whose fortnight in the Ellucero Swamps is a model of its kind, even without its unprecedented bonus of free quinine.

Perhaps at this point I ought to give a clearer sketch of my comrades in the enterprise. The scientific attainments of Professor Summerlee are too well known for me to trouble to recapitulate them, especially as the 26-part programme based on the serialisations in the *Sunday Times* of the book adapted from his film of his three weeks with the fig-eating sloths of El Salvador is already gripping audiences throughout the world. His tall, gaunt figure is insensible to fatigue (he has been known to give eleven interviews in a single day), and his dry, sardonic manner is uninfluenced by any change in his surroundings and is, indeed, written into his contracts. He loses no opportunity to manifest his contempt for our leader, Professor Challenger, maintaining that no scientist worthy of the title can be expected to serve under the leadership of a man prepared to travel to BBC Bristol to do *The Living World* on sound only, for twenty pounds a time. Further, Professor Summerlee firmly believed we were all embarked upon a wild-goose chase, and had it not been for the fact that his forthcoming book, *Great Wild-Goose Chases Of Our Time*, had already earned him a record £100,000 advance from Readers Digest Condensed Books before condensation, he would at that very moment have been lecturing to the Annual Conference of Methodist Accountants in South Bend, Indiana.

Lord John Roxton has some points in common with Professor Summerlee, and others in which they are the very antithesis of one another. A botanist who rose to prominence through his endorsement of Bio-Miracle, the houseplant food which took Britain by storm until a Venus Flytrap raised on it ran amok and ate an airedale, Lord John subsequently chaired the popular BBC 1 panel game, *Smear Test*, before becoming an international figure overnight with his adaptation of the Eskimo mime-play *Grass*, a symbolist drama concerned with ecology and newly set in a middle-class NW1 socialist household, which ran in the Peter Brooke version for five years before being filmed simultaneously by both Ken Russell and Lindsay Anderson.

Of Sir Solly Challenger, little need be said. A friend to both main parties, the only microbiologist to have negotiated with Ian Smith, a Chairman of the Arts Council whose study of the weasel ran to five impressions in Penguin and whose study of the penguin ran to five editions in Weasel, what finer leader could we have sought? Happy was I, as we abseiled down into the Great Hole of Venezuela, to be roped beneath so great a personality!

We touched bottom at noon on the 21st, a triumph marred only by a knife fight between the Features Bookings Managers of BBC TV and Yorkshire Television, on the grounds that the feet of Professor Challenger, who was contracted exclusively to BBC, had been shot by Yorkshire cameramen while taking pictures of the descent of Lord John, who was exclusively contracted to *them*, and who, to complicate matters further, had insisted on waving his bottle of whisky, label uppermost, at the same moment as Professor Summerlee was attempting to wave *his* bottle of gin; with the result that a second fracas immediately broke out between the rival distillers' agents.

It was at this fraught moment that an iguanodon came past; but, unhappily, when this was pointed out to Summerlee by an excited Challenger, Summerlee snapped back: 'Sod your effing iguanodon, what about my gin?', which meant that the unique alarm cry of the iguanodon, never before heard by man, had to be erased from the tape because of the impermissible language counterpointing it. We never saw an iguanodon again.

Worse was to come.

It was towards three p.m. that afternoon that tragedy struck. With an initiative which belied his young years, one of the junior members of our party who had qualified to join it on the strength of a recent first-class honours degree in biochemistry from Cambridge but who, we discovered too late, had used it to gain an executive position with a leading copywriting agency, had arranged to have lowered, from a helicopter hired earlier in Caracas, a small family saloon drawn from a new Japanese range. The emphasis of the sales promotion was to be laid upon its durability and toughness; and our young colleague had devised the slogan: A DINOSAUR COULD TREAD ON IT! This in fact proved to be true; a dinosaur could not only tread on it, but at seven minutes before three o'clock, a dinosaur did tread on it.

We put our young colleague in a foolscap envelope, and resolved, when time permitted, to give him a Christian burial.

The terrible affair cast, inevitably, a pall of gloom on the entire party. Many of us had brought along similar, though smaller, products in order to test them under these novel and eye-catching conditions—I myself had imported a kettle of polyurethane gloss and a small table-top to demonstrate the paint's imperviousness to the weightiest tread—but it was clear that dinosaurs were far heavier than we had anticipated; and when Lord John's new wool-substitute thornproof hacking-jacket in lovat Roxtonette was pecked to shreds in seconds by a pleistocene wren, thereby wiping out a world-wide sales campaign geared to the coming autumn, there were many among us who would then and there have called off the entire expedition. Professor Challenger's iron will, however, prevailed; and when, soon after supper, the group of which he owns eighty per cent, Black Diplodocus, waxed their first single to a haunting counterpoint of ornithischian shrieking and his A & R man pronounced it fantastic, our spirits rose again.

The first night passed virtually without incident, although some of us were kept awake by Summerlee's aldis lamp, by which he was morsing copy to an *Observer Colour Supplement* secretary leaning over the crater's rim, a thousand feet up. Nor was dawn the lovely thing it normally is in this region, awoken as we were to the stench from the pot in which a leading TV gourmet was researching a chapter for her *Saurian Cookbook*. There is something about the odour given off by a triceratops head simmering on a low light which can only be described as indescribable.

But the rest of the day went remarkably well. How benevolently Dame Fortune can smile when the desire moves her! Who would ever have guessed that I, a person of no great moment in this world, should have been granted the boon of being the first human being ever to set eyes upon two bronto-saurases mating, a spread worth twenty thousand dollarsworth of *Playboy's* money any day of the week, not to mention second rights to *Paris Match* and *Stern*? And, miracle upon miracles, joy upon joys, also have had the luck to come upon Henry! Or, since the scientific record must be kept impeccable, to have Henry come upon me, Henry whose magnificent pterodacty-lian ugliness has since been reproduced on a million Henry tea-towels and carrier bags, whose incredibly revolting body has formed the basis of a soft toy industry in which I am the ma-jority shareholder, Henry whose birdfood sales to date have outstripped not only Arthur the cat, but also every performing animal that ever lived, Henry whose TV puppet *doppelgänger* now bobs and nods in every living-room in the civilised world— Henry whose strong claws fastened in my shoulders upon that fateful afternoon and whose strong leathery wings bore me up and out of that fearful place, a clear week ahead of the schedu-led heli-lift and thus a clear week ahead of the opposition, whom I left baying and gesticulating in the grotty green depths below!

Where, for all I know, they still remain. There has been no word these several months; and I can only assume that the blanket coverage afforded me by a grateful commercial world has left my colleagues with nothing to sell, and, moreover, per-suaded those who had previously committed themselves to hau-ling them from the abyss for subsequent profit will have considered the inadvisability of flooding the market, and let sleeping dogs lie.

An Open Letter to Alexander Solzhenitsyn

MY DEAR ALEXANDER:

I hope you will forgive me for not having written sooner; but I know that I do not have to explain to you, of all men, how it is sometimes with writers, that clattering of the heart when the sought words elude and you cannot be sure that they will ever come again, that chill greasy fear in the endless waking hours of the night that perhaps it is the mind itself that has gone, that crushing pressure always to anatomise each minutia, each new refraction of the psyche, to place it in its inner context of the soul, and its outer context of society, with unimpeachable precision, always concentrating, always articulating, not to mention where the fence blew down the week before last and neighbour's refusal to restore same, despite arris-rails clearly visible on his side, plus car failing MOT on account of Excessive Play In Front Trunnions, also having to take Percy up the vet for spring worming, while at same time working out Deductible Input Tax For This Period (Partly Exempt Persons Should Also See Box 24) set against Percentage Used To Attribute Input Tax (Box 14 x 100 divided by Box 16), together with small daughter forcing Panda down lav, first sign of which being flushwater turning bathroom into ornamental pond due to stuffed arm stuck in S-bend (with aid of torch, can see glass eye staring back up at me from unreachable depths), and how do you get a plumber Sundays?

Anyway, Alexander Isayevich, every time I switched on the television set during those fraught periods of writer's block that tend to start clogging the mind a few minutes before *Colditz, Match Of The Day, The Pallisers, Colombo, The World At War, Pot Black, Parkinson,* and *Panorama* (not to mention *Jackanory, Farmer's World* and *Nai Zindagi Naya Jeevan*), there was your fraught beloved face staring out of some bulletin or flash, mugging to lensmen across a bald sea of agents and publishers.

Either that, or they were serialising Raymond Massey's *Abraham Lincoln*.

And every time those lugubrious eyes peered out at me from the fringing bristle, guilt welled up within me at my continuing omission. Must dash off a note to old Alexander, I would say to myself, welcome him to the West, extend the hand of literary fraternity, give him a few tips, enclose a couple of quid for nibs and blodge, well, I've been down on my luck myself before now, haven't I?

And now it is probably too late. For I have just caught sight of a tucked-away item in tonight's *Evening Standard*, which runs, in toto: 'Exiled Soviet writer Alexander Solzhenitsyn may not settle in Norway because the tax laws would mean he might pay up to fifty per cent tax on his Swiss bank account deposits'.

So there it is, Alexander, out of the Communist frying-pan and into the Capitalist fire, and the snow not yet slid from your welts. One moment it's the KGB kicking the doorknobs off in the small hours, the next it's crack teams of Scandinavian revenue men with rimless specs and immaculate clipboards intimating that it's either an immediate fifty pee in the £ or chuck the belongings back into the red-spotted hankie and ring up a mini-cab for Oslo Airport.

It won't improve, either. I gather that your next choice is Switzerland, if they'll let you; and though the tax hammer is, granted, less sledgy, I doubt that the racked Soviet soul is likely to settle snugly among the alpine slopes a-teem with resident millionaire paperback hacks, drunken film-stars, racing drivers, refugee investment analysts, elderly Tory peers, and all the raucous effluvia of less stable European economies, not to mention the Swiss themselves, who tend to blink a lot, if they're the communicative sort, but otherwise constitute an unfertile sod for the authorial rhizome.

There's always Ireland, no tax at all, and a lot of green. But while their total tax concession to writers appears on the face of it generous, they have had some difficulty, as you may know, in determining who is a writer and who not, and are almost certainly, with typical Irish precision, using the rule of thumb which says that if a bloke is lying in a Dublin gutter with a bottle of Guinness in each pocket, no collar, and a four-day growth of stubble, and conducting himself in *The Wild Colonial Boy* with a grubby baton made from the rolled-up manuscript of his unpublished first novel, then he it is who constitutes the literary norm; and, somehow, that is not a part I see you comfortably playing.

France allows resident writers two tax-free years, but the toll exacted, socially, for the financial benefit is heavy: the literary establishment would reject you on the grounds that you had never written a novel entitled *A Rock, A Tree, A Chair* and running to either (a) five thousand words, or (b) five million words; and the intellectual establishment would reject you on the grounds that you knew nothing about (a) Communism, or (b) Alfred Hitchcock.

Spain is clearly out. Nor do I see you, Alexander Isayevich, conforming to the German requirements, which demand either that you live on a derelict farm a hundred miles from anywhere and write about very, very simple things, like hens, or else run for the Bundestag. The tax is murder, too.

Well, yes, all right, so it is in England. But, that aside, the benefits here are limitless, reducing the Inland Revenue's encroachments to negligibility. Pre-eminent among the wonderful advantages is the fact that, whereas these other European sanctuaries will require you to write, will scrutinise each emergent line for signs of growth or decay, will constantly be calling you to account in the slabby pages of their myriad literary magazines and newspapers for any slight deviation from the total commitment expected of you, in England *you will not need to write at all!*

You will only have to *have* written; and with a fair few pages under the belt and a framed Nobel cheque nailed up beside the flying ducks, your qualifications are irreproachable. In England, once he *has* written, the writer's life begins in earnest.

You will never be out of a studio for long, radio or telly: in a dark woollen shirt and a dark woollen tie, you will sit on chromium deck-chairs, semi-circled with a Catholic peer and an articulate musician and a West Indian social worker and a critic who paints a bit or plays the piano a bit, and a pale (but still lovely) girl who has written a virtually unpunctuated trilogy about being a pale (but still lovely) girl, and you will discuss things. All manner of things: the spoliation of the Dorset coastline, the threat of *Deep Throat* to all we hold most dear, supermarkets and the dehumanisation of shopping, battered wives, the initial teaching alphabet, tower blocks, Watergate, What Does The Future Really Hold For The Third World, pets, God, and the licensing laws.

You will generate millions of words, but write none. There will be interviews showing how you have found happiness in a Green Belt executive home, possibly by knocking two internal walls down and converting the loft into a combined darkroom and play-area; and interviews revealing that a life of roulette, elite discos and tall women is no substitute In A Writer's Life for the stability of a happy marriage and your children's continuing wonder at the unfolding world, which you can share; and interviews discussing parking-meters and the concomitant erosion of civil liberties; and interviews At Fifty, At Sixty, and even, if your luck holds, At Sixty-Three and -Four. There will be a lot of money in these interviews, Alexander Isayevich.

There may also be fat contracts to stand beside a dog and sell tasty liver morsels; sip vodka with no more than a silent wink to camera during the pre-Christmas sales-peak; take down from a rosewoodette shelf Volume One of The Complete Winston Churchill bound in rich washable rubbishene.

There will be your name up there in giant capitals: VERY SOLZHENITSYN. VERY SANDERSON.

There will even be wonderful opportunities to act as Script Adviser to the BBC's ninety-eight part serialisation of *Engels In Love*, which means the producer rings you up once a month to enquire whether it's Leningrad that's on the Volga, or is he thinking of Stalingrad, if it's still called that, ha-ha-ha?

There will be wonderful literary parties in Belgrave Square and Gloucester Crescent, where the literary talk will make your very being thrill with its intense and passionate involvement with First Pakistani Serial Rights, and possibilities of adaptation for the Belgian broadcasting services, and a whole chain of speaking engagements in Wisconsin.

So I urge you, Alexander Isayevich, praying that it is still not too late, to reconsider your remaining years: do you really want some bleak and insistent foreign refuge, where you will be compelled to lean across a desk, day in, day out, night in, night out, thinking, thinking, thinking, and scribbling, scribbling,

scribbling, page after page, book after book?

Or would you rather not, for the tiny price of a one-way air-ticket, escape to England and become a Writer?

Bloody Criminal

'Scotland Yard has evidence that teams of pickpockets working for the Mafia entered Britain last month. They are far more skilled than British pickpockets. Following the recent invasion by expert foreign shoplifters, this trend cannot but be disturbing.' — Sunday Telegraph

A MALEVOLENT WIND WHIPPED the sleet across the roof of St. Jude's, Lewisham, lashing the east flanks of two men in flat caps and mufflers struggling for a handhold with their sodden wooly mittens. It was three in the morning, and there was no moon.

'I can't see a bleeding thing!' shrieked the first man, into the gale. 'Give us the torch!'

The second man groped in his knap-sack. Sandwiches scattered, and were hurled, fragmenting, across SE13. A thermos flask rolled down the roof, and exploded on the pavement beneath. Dogs began to bark.

'Bloody sandwiches!' cried the first man. 'Bloody coffee! We din't come up here for an early bleeding lunch!'

'You got to 'ave sunnink to keep out the cold!' muttered the second man. 'Get a chill on the liver, where are you? You panic, that's your trouble. I've broke me digestive biscuits now.'

'The torch!' shouted the first man.

'All this hollering,' muttered the second man, 'there'll be law all over in a minute.'

'Just give us the torch!'

'I was coming to that,' said the second man. 'I think I left it on the sideboard.'

'What!'

'Either that,' said the second man, 'or in the lav. We got a bulb gone. You can't see to pull the wossname.'

'My God,' moaned the first man, 'we got a roofload of lead up 'ere, and we can't even see it!'

'Go by feel,' said the second man.

They took their mittens off.

'Give us the chisel,' said the first man. 'I've got a seam.'

He dug for a while. He stopped. He held his hand up to his face.

'I thought so,' he snarled. 'This is a sodding spoon!'

The second man took it back.

'No good blaming me,' he said. 'Got frostbite, haven't I? Numb. Can't feel nothing. We ought to get proper gloves. Them thin kid jobs. Worth laying out on them. Ex-naval officers. Here's the chisel.'

The first man snatched it, laid it under the thick edge of lead, prised. The blade snapped off, and fell into the night. They peered after it.

'Sheffield, that was,' said the first man. 'Can't understand it.'

'OY!' roared a voice below.

'It's fallen on a bloody copper,' said the second man.

At 3.30 am, they were taken to Lewisham Police Station and charged.

At 3.45 am, a black Mercedes three-tonner drew up outside the church. Four Germans got out. They were wearing black insulated rubber suits, black rubber gloves, and Oster-Darmführ black climbing boots, and carrying a rocket-powered grapnel to which was attached a fine nylon rope, and two battery-driven, cold-blade cutters. Each of their helmets bore a tiny pin-pointing light.

By 4.45, the van had gone.

And inside the church, the first drops of icy drizzle were beginning to darken the altar-cloth.

'M'Lud,' said the defence counsel, smiling at the jury, who, confused, smiled back, 'I submit that since the chief prosecution witness has been unable to support the charge of rape with any evidence whatsoever, *including her own testimony*, then the jury has no option but to find my client not guilty.'

'It's a lie!' screamed a young woman in a floral hat from the well of the court. 'I know he done it! It was just what with him being so quick, so clever with his hands and everything, I mean,

101

I didn't start thinking about it till he'd got back in the milkfloat and gone off. I only asked him in on account of sparrows pecking holes in the gold tops.'

'Silence!' roared the judge.

The defendant, resplendent in chocolate chalk-stripe, diamante tie-pin, spats, and two-tone shoes, merely picked his magnificent row of alabaster teeth with a gold toothpick, and smiled the faintest of Italian smiles beneath his waxed wisp of moustache.

'No sign of a struggle, no cries, no complaints from neighbours, how do we know the defendant was even in the house at all?' appealed the barrister.

'Is true wotty say,' murmured the defendant, flashing a dark eye.

The jury retired for two minutes, after which the defendant set his beige fedora at a raffish angle, and strolled out into the sunshine, twirling his gold-topped cane.

Honest Nat Ginsberg emerged from a concealed door at the back of Walthamstow dog track, and walked cautiously across the car park to his waiting Bentley. He was carrying, as he always did, a Gladstone bag so stuffed with notes that the squeak of its straining clasp sang above the heavy homeward shuffle of the dispirited punters.

He had just drawn abreast of the car when two large citizens in stocking masks sprang out at him from behind a neighbouring Cortina. The first swung a loose punch at the bookmaker's head, missed, and drove his fist into the side of the Bentley. As he doubled, shrieking, his partner (who had leapt forward to snatch the Gladstone bag), fell across him and, off balance, was pole-axed by the short left jab which Honest Nat kept by him at all times for medicinal purposes.

However, so preoccupied were the trio with their own various ineptitudes, they did not notice a tiny lemon-faced figure slide out of the gloaming until he stood in front of Honest Nat, bowed politely from the waist, and felled him with a single (and effortless) karate chop.

He stooped, and picked up the fallen bag.

'So solly,' he said.

''E's not Solly,' croaked one of the British muggers, pulling himself upright on the Bentley. 'Must be a case of mistaken identity, squire, ha-ha-ha, give us the bag.'

The Jap bowed again.

'How you like bloken leg, latface?' he enquired politely.

And, stepping over the supine ruin of the other mugger, he slipped back into the encircling night as silently as he had come.

The green fog hung heavy on Whitechapel. Down the mean, invisible streets, a bent figure hobbled, the mildewed tatter of his old opera cloak hugged about him, the dented topper bobbing on his skinny brow. In one hand he clutched a mahogany box of surgical instruments, in the other a coil of silken cord. His emphysemic breath wheezed out in little excited puffs, and oily moisture gleamed on his anticipating cheeks.

It was as he turned the final corner into Cable Street that a fearful female scream penetrated the night, and ebbed on an awful wheeze. He stopped, shaking with fury, and as he did so, a bicycle rattled past. He could not see it, nor the man who rode it, but it went by him in a reek of Gauloise smoke, accompanied by the unmistakable lyrics of *Auprès De Ma Blonde* sung in a heavy Basque baritone.

The Ripper sighed, and turned on his heel, and, in a single movement, hurled both box and rope into the fog. He was a hundred and thirty now, and he could not take the competition any more.

Take the Wallpaper in the Left Hand and the Hammer in the Right . . .

YOU LIVE WITH A WOMAN for ten years, not an intimacy remains unshared, and where are you?

It was Christmas morning, possibly with a capital M, so auspicious was the time, and the house re-echoed to the Yuley joy of children breaking their new toys over one another. Since dawn, the air had been filled with flying cogs, the walls of the upstairs hall shone with new day-glo graffiti, and on the stairs the pitiful shards of model soldier lay thick as on the field of Omdurman, their little swords and broken rifles still game for a last kamikaze jab at the bare parental sole as it lurched, hungover, through the inimical pile towards the reviving caffeine.

I hobbled eventually to a breakfast table that would have left Oliver Wendell Holmes himself speechless. A doll's eye glared up from the porridge, rubber insects were all over the toast, and beside the coffee-pot stood the remains of an electric dog. Cobbled together in far Nippon by deft saffron digits, the animal had been a masterpiece of delicate invention a half-hour earlier, when my small daughter first flung herself at its wrappings. In theory, when you pulled its leash, two batteries in its cunningly hollowed bowels sprang into energy, and its little tail wagged while its little legs waddled it forward and its little head nodded as its little mouth yapped.

In practice, however, you pull its leash, and a little tin flange clicks up and down obscenely in its hindquarters, the tail having fallen off, and its little legs waddle it forward at a slow limp; but its little head does not nod, because its little head is now on the other side of the table. The decapitated torso, in fact, is crawling towards its severed skull, and, illogically, barking at it. As the high point of a Hammer film, the thing now has few equals, but as a cuddly toy it has all the winsome appeal of a clockwork boil.

I was still staring at the furry wreckage and musing on the whims of economic history whereby Japan's fiduciary sun was allowed to rise on such insubstantial collateral as this, when I heard my wife say: 'Never mind, you'll be able to mend all their toys now.'

How shall I describe the nudgy emphasis of that *NOW*? She is a subtle girl, and when she slips into italics, every hackle I have tells me there are difficult times ahead.

'I'm sorry?' I riposted wittily.

'You haven't opened your present,' she said.

'Oh!' I cried, having practised; and having painstakingly ignored the large parcel beside my chair which contained a half doz shirts, at the very least, possibly a brace of sweaters, and who knew how many ties, cravats, matching foulards? What the sequitur might be bridging them to the dismembered doggie, I could not begin to guess; but it had been a pretty heavy night, and I might well have lost a syllogistic rivet or two along the way.

I threw my remains upon the parcel and, having broken a forenail on the knot and gashed a thumb on the paper (co-ordination is one of my shorter suits: I am one of the few men I know to bang his head on seven-foot lintels), I came to a book. A book with a lock and a handle on it, yet.

'Hurrah,' I murmured. I brightened. Shirts it wasn't, but a *fake* book it might well be, a piece of snappy packaging for the literary cigar-smoker, say, under which head I fall.

'It's like a little suitcase,' I said.

'Isn't it, though?' she replied. 'What an eye for detail you have, and all self-taught.'

Detecting a coppery tang of disappointment here, and instantly tracing its source, I cranked up my enthusiasm a couple of notches.

'Wow!' I cried, hefting the bogus vol, 'How exciting to have a package *within* a package! Ha-ha-ha, it's passing itself off as—let me see—*The Readers Digest Complete Do-It-Yourself Manual*!'

'Is it?' she said.

'Isn't it?' I replied.

I snapped back the catch, and opened it, and it contained a

million or two loose-leaf pages, cleverly ring-bound for maximum inaccessibility. They fell open at a page of circular saws.

'Oh, look,' I said, 'circular saws.'

'There you are,' she cried happily, 'and you've always maintained you weren't technical.'

'I can, however, recognise any tool you care to name,' I replied. 'I have learned to, just as mice come to learn about mousetraps. It is almost an instinct with me, now.'

'It will be a whole new skill,' she countered. 'With this book, anyone can learn how to build anything. Look,' she continued, turning a leaf with enviable dexterity, 'a sideboard! All you do is saw wood up and fit it together.'

'Well, well! And think of all the fuss they made of Sheraton!' Many things were seething in my head at this moment, the least of them being my utter ineptitude when faced with anything constructional. The only thing I ever succeeded in making in school woodwork, and that after a year of rib-tickling failed attempts, was a toast-rack, and even then you had to put a rubber band around the toast to keep the whole thing from falling apart. I transferred to metalwork after that, where they would give me steel plates which I turned into shrapnel. But this drear practical record, as I say, was nothing to the deeper significances with which the gift was fraught.

'Darling,' I said, 'I had always believed that you thought of me as a sophisticated homme du monde, dashing scourge of croupiers and sommeliers alike, a two-fisted wit over whom lissom dollies sighed and suffered, a young god who could hold his liquor and his own with Freddie Ayer! Look here, upon this picture, and on this—and how many joiners do you know who could hit you with an apt Shakespearian reference at this early hour?—and tell me what you see.'

She looked at the proffered page. A man in a leather apron was demonstrating the correct method of squinting at a rebating plane. He had several ball-points in an upper pocket, no doubt of different hues, and a short-back-and-sides he had clearly manufactured himself, possibly with adze and chisel.

'Is that,' I cried, 'how you see me? A shaper of matchless dovetails, an adroit recycler of cotton-reels, a host to keep his guests enthralled, as they sip their Emva Cream, with tales of tile and bookcase? You know me,' I hurtled on, 'the only craft I have is gluing, and that imperfect. We have shared a life for ten years, you have watched me glue shelves to walls, and seen them fall, you have lain awake and listened while glued slates detached themselves from the roof, you have reeled back as wardrobe doors came unstuck from their hinges—and at the end of it all, *this*?'

'It's just a question of the proper tools,' she said, 'saws and chisels and—things.'

'Wounds is the word you were looking for,' I said, 'that is what goes with saws and chisels, a floorful of thumbs, the squirt of arteries, overworked surgeons converting my body into a Fair Isle masterpiece!'

Whereupon, wordless, she shoved back her chair, and left.

I sat for a while, staring at the table (how did they fit the legs in, how did they get the top on, to what arcane glue secrets were cabinetmakers privy?) and the ruined toys, and I thought: would it not, in truth, be cool to wave mystic implements over these remains, bring old British skills to bear upon Jap tattiness, return the toys, new-perfect, to the kids and accept their squeals of joy and love? Or knock up—I flipped the book—a cocktail cabinet or two, some bunk beds, even a summer house? Put in (page 41) a swimming-pool, relay the parquet floors, convert the loft?

Would this infringe upon the image of Renaissance Man? On the contrary, it would enhance it, endow new facets, why, I could paint the Mona Lisa with my left hand while my right was inventing the helicopter! I would buy gorblimey trousers, a crusty briar, learn how to hold nails in my mouth and tell the consistency of cement by the smell alone, and gawping neighbours would come to point out the matchless gabling, the new storey, the fresh bow windows—

I rushed out, borne on the boiling enthusiasm, into the garage which was to be my workshop, carrying the manual by its handle (perhaps, now, I should always carry it with me, and when crowds formed around some fallen masonry or shattered window or the torn woodwork of a bomb-blasted pub, I would elbow them aside, holding it aloft and crying 'Let me through, I'm a handyman!'), and, as luck would have it, there in an old tobacco tin on the window ledge I found a threaded hook, just the thing to hang the book on for easy reference, so I screwed it into the plaster, and I found a piece of string, and I looped it through the handle, and I hung the book up on the wall, *and it did not fall off!*

Until I slammed the garage door, that is.

I looked through the window, and there seemed to be a lot of plaster on the floor. But it did not faze me. A little thing like fallen plaster doesn't bother me any more.

Why, I'll have it glued back up any day now.

A Walk on the Short Side

Afflicted cops are big box-office. As the crippled Ironside wheels himself off-screen after six record-breaking years, blind Longstreet taps on to take his place in fifty million homes on both sides of the Atlantic. And when he goes . . .?

THEY PULLED THE STIFF OUT of the East River at 3.02 am. From the knees downwards he was concrete, from the neck up he was space. They found the shotgun in a trashcan at the corner of 88th and 3rd. It went down to forensic at 6.41. At 7.12 it was on the Commissioner's desk. He was a big man to be involved. But it was a big case. They'd had six DOA's with the same MO's in the past six days. The press was on the Department's neck.

'Our first break,' said forensic. 'All the previous MW's were clean. This one, all but.'

The Commissioner turned the murder weapon in his hands. 'All but?'

'No prints, no blood, no hairs, no threads, no number, no ID.'

'That's the all,' said the Commissioner. 'Now the but.'

Forensic held a tiny plastic envelope to the desklight.

'Dandruff,' he said. 'On the right barrel.'

They looked at one another, for a long second. The Commissioner reached for his red phone.

'Get Sidestreet up here!' he snapped.

The door opened, and they looked for him. Sometimes Sidestreet would come into a room and you wouldn't know he was there for an hour. That's the way it is when you're three-feet-two. It was pretty short for a New York cop, especially in Homicide; but he hadn't always been three-two. Once he'd been six-feet-one. That was before Joe 'Fettucini' Verde had taken him

109

for a little ride and dumped his Chevy in the Jersey car-crusher. The Verde mob stood by laughing while the car went through. Then they stopped laughing. As it fell off the dumper, the trunk opened and Sidestreet got out. He pulled his snub-nose .45 (it had been a long-barrel .32 when he got in) and dropped three of the Verde gang with his first clip.

That was when the Commissioner knew he had a cop on his staff.

'What's up, Chief?' said Sidestreet.

The Commissioner winced. Even across a big room, the legendary Sidestreet breath was enough to strip the chrome off your badge. Discreetly, forensic took a mask from his surgical coat, and slipped it on.

'Got a lead on the East Side killings,' said the Commissioner. 'We found dandruff on the scatter-gun. Here!'

He threw the little envelope, and Sidestreet caught it. He breathed it open. He looked.

'You're a dandruff man,' said the Commissioner, 'maybe you——'

'Come again,' said Sidestreet, twiddling a knob on his chest. 'These goddam batteries!'

'YOU'RE A DANDRUFF SUFFERER!' roared the Commissioner. 'I THOUGHT YOU COULD GET SOMETHING FROM IT!'

'Yeah,' said Sidestreet. 'You can get conjunctivitis. It's an infection, on account of the scurf gets in your eyes. I had it years. What happens is——'

'I didn't mean that,' said the Commissioner. 'I meant, you know, like you could get information from this sample, right?'

'Sure,' said Sidestreet. 'I been getting treatment down the Nu-Hair Follicle Clinic And Sauna. Also for the alopecia. I seen this dandruff down there. Comes off a tall wop with a wall-eye. We use the same oculist, also. Don't know him too good, on account of his right eye looks to the left and my left eye looks to the right. Most days we don't see each other at all, even when we're, you know, standing right next to each other. Which barrel was the dandruff on?'

'The right,' said forensic, through his mask.

'That figures,' said Sidestreet. 'This wop's a left-hander. The right barrel's against his cheek, right? The dandruff probably drops outa these long wop sideburns he's got.'

110

'Name?' snapped the Commissioner.

Sidestreet shrugged.

'Who knows? Nobody talks to me, Chief, you know that. Even my dentist works with a three-foot probe. Gimme the mug shots.'

At 9.05 they had a name.

'Pick him up,' said the Commissioner.

Sidestreet's specially converted wagon wailed uptown. Bullet-proof and radar-equipped, it also had no seats in the back so that Sidestreet could stand up, on account of the haemorrhoids, and a specially tailored mini-urinal in pastel blue near-porcelain, for his enuresis. In the early days, a lot of hoods got away due to the fact that by the time Sidestreet's standard police car found a public lavatory and by the time Sidestreet had found a dime and by the time he'd come out onto the street again, the fugitive car was halfway across New Mexico with new plates, and full beards on the occupants.

'Don't pick it, boss!'

Sidestreet dropped his hand instantly from his barber's rash: he relied too much on trusty, warm-hearted Police-Nurse Rona Kowalski SRN, the best colonic irrigator east of the Pecos, ever to put her nose out of joint. Even though his osteopath was a household word wherever arthritics gathered, and a nose to him was as a parking violator to Sidestreet.

'I'm nervous, Kowalski,' said Sidestreet, 'that's all.'

'I can tell, boss,' she said. 'When we slowed for that last red light, I could hear your eczema crackling.'

'I never ran in a fellow scurfnik before,' said Sidestreet. 'The nearest I ever came was when we trapped Mad Nat Dolfuss in Palisades Park and shot it out. It wasn't till we got him down to the morgue and took his clothes off that I realised him and me had athlete's foot in all the same places.' Sidestreet looked away, sighing. 'It made me feel—I dunno—dirty, somehow.'

The wagon came around the corner into 110th Street, and slammed into the kerb. Sidestreet sprang out, deaf-aid swinging, a pack of regulation laxatives in his left hand, and his nickel-plated ear-syringe in his right, ready for anything. Pausing only for a short nose-bleed on the step, he pocketed his dentures, and leapt through the doorway of a peeling brownstone.

He dropped to one knee, almost imperceptibly.

'Okay, Zucchini, we know you're in there!' cried Sidestreet.

There was no answer from the dark passage.

'Don't gimme that, Zucchini, I seen the dandruff! People like us shouldn't fit navy blue carpet. *This here's fresh scurf!* Also, you forget I'm a non-tall person—us non-talls develop special senses to compensate. I ain't as far away from these little white flakes as most people!'

'Okay, Sidestreet, I'm coming out!'

Sidestreet squinted into the gloom. It was the way he looked at everything.

'How'd you know it's me, Zucchini?'

'You kidding?' The voice was faint. 'Tear-gas I can take. Mace I inhale. But—for Chrissake, Sidestreet, don't your best friends tell you *anything*?'

'Cops,' muttered Sidestreet, 'don't have best friends.'

He was still reflecting upon this, when the killer sprang out of the darkness. In an instant, Sidestreet was on his feet. He swung a short left to the shin, followed it with a right uppercut to the knee, and was about to take off for a crippling groin-butt when he suddenly let out a cry of agony and fell to the floor. Zucchini tore himself free and disappeared down the steps, almost knocking over PN Kowalski who was rushing in with iron lungs, wooden legs, surgical trusses, glass eyes, stomach pumps, vitamin pills, wigs, throat-sprays, varicose stockings and all the other essential kit carried in Sidestreet's wagon in case of emergencies.

'What is it, boss?' she shrieked. 'Where'd he get you?'

Sidestreet looked up at her, his fine squat face creased with pain.

'My arches,' he gasped, 'they just fell!'

Sidestreet jumped up and down furiously and shook the walls of his cot until the entire orthopaedic ward rattled.

'I'm okay I tellya, Chief!' he cried. 'They fixed the arches, also my trick knee, adenoids, ingrowing toenails, both, and they say the psoriasis will clear up as soon as I stop worrying about my hernia. I want out!'

'Nothing doing, Sidestreet,' barked the Commissioner. 'You're livebait!'

'How's that?' muttered Sidestreet, turning both channels up full and cutting in his tweeter.

'You heard,' said the Commissioner. 'Turns out Zucchini is one of the Verde mob. You're the only one who can put a finger on him, Sidestreet, so sure as hell they're gonna try and eliminate you. I got the entire hospital staked out.'

Sidestreet relaxed.

'A job,' he said. 'That's different.' He patted his pillow. 'Good job I keep a little something by me, Chief. For medicinal purposes, heh-heh-heh!'

'Good luck, Sidestreet,' said the Commissioner, and left.

At 10 pm, the nurse settled Sidestreet for sleep.

At 10.30, the lights went out.

At 11.15, two men in white coats and stethoscopes slid up the ward, and stopped at Sidestreet's bed.

'Okay, cop, issa where you getta yours!' hissed the nearer.

Sidestreet, eyes closed, slid a hand beneath his pillow, slowly. There was nothing there.

'Iffa you lookin' for your gun,' said the other hood, 'you canna forget it. Thissa night nurse,' he laughed nastily, 'issa personal frien'.'

Whereupon he drew a silenced Walther, took aim on Sidestreet's sweating forehead, and fell over.

The second torpedo looked at him for a couple of seconds, closed his eyes, and slid to the floor beside him.

Half a minute later, the ward was full of cops. A frenzied Commissioner appeared at Sidestreet's bed.

'Thank God you're all right!' he cried. 'Dear Heaven, Sidestreet, you got them both! And we found your gun on the night nurse—how in God's name . . .'

'They just came close,' said Sidestreet, 'and pow! That was it.'

'But how?'

Sidestreet shrugged.

'Could be yellow fever,' he said. 'Could be bubonic plague, smallpox, hepatitis. Could be typhoid, TB, cholera, could be——' he smiled '——hell, you know me, Commissioner. It could be anything.'

The Tourists Karamazov

'*More and more Soviet citizens are catching the travel bug. Last year 2,100,000 of them went abroad, 900,000 to capitalist countries. The bulk of the increase comes from package-deal tourists.*' – Daily Telegraph

ON A BITTERLY HOT MORNING towards the end of July, 197–, a young man whose skin was the colour of a boiled saveloy left his little room at the top of the El Diabolico Hotel that lay lost among the cranes and half-dug building sites of Torremolinos, and began to descend the step-worn stairs.

On every landing, he passed the little knots of fellow-guests huddled around the silent lift-doors, clutching their frail GUM shrimpnets and staring disconsolately into the dark shaft, some upwards, some downwards. As he padded quickly past them, his terror of meeting anybody would suddenly lurch in his trembling bowel as first this one, now that, would turn their stricken eyes towards him. Sometimes, they spoke.

'Good morning, Alexei Alexeyovich,' they might say, 'the elevator has still not arrived. It has been three days. Some of the children are faint from lack of water.'

Whenever he could, he would merely stare at them, perhaps nod; but when it could not be avoided (when some elderly grandmother, perhaps, lay on the stairs, rocking her head-scarved head and moaning softly, blocking his escape), he would reply:

'Why do you not come down the stairs like me? It seems very possible that the elevator has broken down.'

At which the men would shake their heads, and say:

'We have had no official notice that the elevator has ceased to function. It is set out clearly in the official brochure that there is an elevator to carry guests to the lower floors. There is nothing

114

in the official brochure to indicate that descent by the staircase is allowed.'

'It also states in the official brochure,' the pink young man would reply, 'that there is running hot and cold water. It does not however state that it is running through the ceiling.'

'You are a revanchist parasite, Alexei Alexeyovich,' said a young woman on the second-floor landing, when he gave her this standard reply. 'You are not fit to enjoy the sun-kissed tropical paradise of famed Torremolinos with its many barbecues, its folkloric dancing, its unparalleled shopping, and its paiella, a unique local dish made with prawns and many other fruits of the sea.'

'I observe, Sonya Sonyeova, that you have been studying your official brochure during your holiday outside this elevator. It is clear to me that you do not have hot and cold water running through your ceiling.'

'I do not have a ceiling, filthy Alexei Alexeyovich,' the young woman replied. 'I am in that portion of the internationally-renowned El Diabolico which the beloved comrade workers have seen fit not to complete, no doubt as a protest against fascist oppression. I feel privileged that I have been given the opportunity to share this wonderful moment with them.'

'His head is going all red,' said a little boy beside her. 'What are the running dogs of fascism doing to Alexei Alexeyovich, Sonya Sonyeova?'

'He is changing colour because he is walking about on his own,' said his sister. 'It is my opinion that he is not going on the wonderful air-conditioned buses, each with its own wc, to visit the fabled cathedral of Malaga or take advantage of the streets that have remained unchanged for centuries with their marvellous little shops displaying local woodcraft where you may browse undisturbed but would be foolish not to buy the hand-carved nutcrackers for which the region is famed.'

'I cannot go on the buses, Sonya Sonyeova,' replied Alexei Alexeyovich, 'because they will not leave with three passengers. As everyone on our package-trip is waiting for the lift, with the exception of myself and Mr. and Mrs. Solokilov of Smolensk who are actually sleeping under the bus due to lack of accommodation in the hotel annexe which fell into the sea two nights ago, the drivers are not prepared to leave.'

'I am glad you furnished me with the names of Mr. and Mrs. Solokilov,' said the young woman, writing the names down in her little notebook. 'There is no reason why, simply because they are downstairs already, they should not wait by the lift with everyone else. Where is their solidarity?'

Alexei Alexeyovich sighed, and left them to their pointless vigil, and went down the last two flights to breakfast. It was, like all the others, a lonely meal: the Solokilovs, diminutive in the distance on Table 89, and he alone on Table 3, and between them a vast steppe of white napery vainly awaiting the other 237 packagees. Ten waiters stood by the wall, picking their teeth, and examining their nails. Finally, his own shoved himself upright and slunk across, gripping a cold croissant, bracing himself for the mandatory international bonhomie upon which the management prided itself.

'Georgie Best bloody good, gorblimey,' said the waiter, dropping the croissant onto the young man's plate.

'May I have an egg, please?' said Alexei Alexeyovich, in Russian.

'Thcotland for de Gup,' said the waiter, and shuffled back to the wall.

Alexei Alexeyovich stared after him for a while. He began, for the third time in as many days, to think about complaining; but, as always, as soon as he did so, his hands began to tremble uncontrollably, and the sweat sprang out on his empurpled forehead and began carrying flakes of his skin down his face; he had no proper concept of complaint, he did not even have any real idea of what a management was, it was just that he experienced a far not-quite-familiar stirring of something that made him both excited and uneasy.

He got up instead, and went outside, into the fearful white glare hurtling back off the serried ranks of tower blocks and vast flat expanses of car-park and forecourt. Mr. and Mrs. Solokilov had formed a tiny queue by the front door of their bus. No drivers were to be seen.

'Good morning, Alexei Alexeyovich,' said Solokilov, from whose fur coat steam was gently rising, but which he would not remove as he had been wearing it for his passport photograph, and lived in perpetual terror of any deviation from his official

116

identity. 'We are waiting for the bus to take us to the world-renowned bull-ring of Marbella, playground of princes, because it is Tuesday morning.'

'But the buses will not be going, Grigor Grigorovich,' said the young man, 'because the comrade package is all upstairs waiting for the lift.'

Mr. Solokilov took off his astrakhan hat and removed a saturated timetable from it.

'Tuesday morning, nine a.m., wait by buses for Marbella excursion,' he said, tracing the words with his finger. He put the paper back, and the hat on again.

'Will you not perhaps accompany me to the beach?' said the young man.

'The visit to the beach, its miles of golden sand, its little pools where the crabs play, its parties of gay visitors of every nation, let us pause and listen to the many various tongues, is not until Thursday, Alexei Alexeyovich,' said Mrs. Solokilov.

'After the visit to the glassblowing works,' nodded her husband, 'high in the hills where skilled craftsmen practise the incredible art of their forefathers, note how they suck in before each item, thus avoiding bubbles and flaws.'

He left them there, with a slight bow, and began the long trek across site and dump and slag-heap and rubble and through ruins either half-built or half-demolished, towards the sea. He had never seen the sea; they had all been promised a view of it from the hotel, according to the brochure, but the one balcony from which it was possible to do this (it belonged to the caretaker's penthouse apartment) had fallen off during a light drizzle the week before, and in consequence Alexei Alexeyovich's heart beat a little faster with each forward step, and as the pungency of the ozone seeped, finally, through the fug of diesel and fractured gas mains and frying chips and the massed reek of a million sun-oiled bodies, something not unlike joy took over his entire being. To see the sea, open and unconfined, free and frontierless, irrestrictible and . . .

A hand fell upon his frail shoulder, and he looked round into a pair of iron eyes under a black homburg.

'Come, Alexei Alexeyovich,' said the black homburg.

There was a large Moskva parked at the kerb, with the engine running, and another black homburg inside it.

'Now?' said Alexei Alexeyovich.

'Now. But first you will write on this postcard showing golden funfilled Torremolinos where the elite meet and every day is a holiday.'

'What shall I write?' muttered the young man, as the pen was pushed into his hand.

'You will write: HAVING WONDERFUL TIME. WISH YOU WERE HERE,' said the black homburg, 'and sign it.'

Gunfight at the OK Grill-Room

'High meat prices have made rustling highly lucrative, and it is increasing, says the National Farmers' Union. Livestock worth £30,000 was stolen last year. The NFU said another worrying development was that groups of townsmen were going out with .22 rifles to "kill themselves a sheep".' – Guardian

HE CAME OVER the ridge at sun-up, riding hard. He was tall in the saddle, and lean, and he was the law. He was grey with dust, and the grey was streaked with sweat, like a dry gulch veined briefly with morning dew before it burns off, cracking the parched soil again. It was a long ride out from town. At the top of the ridge, he dismounted, and took off his cycle-clips.

"'Allo," he said, "'allo, 'allo.'

He was a man of few words. But he moved quickly, for a big man.

'Woss,' he said, 'all this, then?'

The two men crouching over the terrible remains looked up. He knew them. They farmed the area. They didn't say anything. They didn't need to. Not with what one of them was holding in his hands.

'That's a sheep's head,' said the lawman.

'That's right,' said the elder farmer.

'Very nice, boiled,' said the lawman. 'With a drop of vinegar.'

'It's the rest of the sheep we're worried about,' said the farmer's son.

'I'd roast that, personally,' said the lawman. 'Saddle, neck, best end, scrag—'

'It's gone,' said the farmer. 'Nothing left but the feet.'

'Ah,' said the lawman. His grey eyes narrowed to slits, and

119

he stared at the bright horizon, thinking hard. 'Soup,' he said, at last.

'What?'

'From the feet. 'Course, you'll have to watch for ticks. Mind you, they tend to float out when it boils.'

The farmer stood up. His jaw was set.

'We want the man,' he said, 'who stole the carcase.'

The lawman took off his helmet, and squinted at the sun, and wiped the sweat from his forehead.

'I understand,' he said. 'There must have been a good forty dinners there.'

And, leaving them to ponder upon these telling words, the tall man threw a long leg over his saddle and rode back towards town.

The saloon fell quiet as his shadow slipped across the floor. Only the consumptive coughing of the hawkfaced doctor slumped at the cribbage-board punctuated the silence, as the sheepmen watched the man in blue walk to the bar, slow and easy.

'Stone's Ginger Wine,' he said.

The blonde barmaid piled her ravishing bust loosely upon the bar, and the thump of her golden heart rattled the glasses on the shelf behind her.

'That's five sheep gone this week, then,' she said.

'In a manner,' said the lawman, 'of speaking.'

'Why is it always bleeding sheep?' cried an embittered old solicitor from a far corner of the room, who had watched rustlers make nonsense of his subsidy from his far Holborn chambers, and had taken the unprecedented step of visiting his property, only to find his flock was a bucket of tails and an old ewe with croup.

'He's right!' exclaimed a young don, whose face was known to millions of TV fans and whose weekend cottage was now a mockery following the theft of the photogenic little lamb that had stood outside it in countless colour supplements. 'Why do they never steal cattle?'

The lawman turned, real slow, and fixed them all with his steely eye.

'What do you think, Doctor?' he said.

120

The hawkfaced man beat his heaving chest. Ash fell from his cigarette. Liquor spilled from his glass. Cards flew from his sleeves.

'There's a lot of it about,' he wheezed at last. 'Take two—wurrgh!—take two aspirins and go to—aaaargh!—bed, and if it's no better, give me a—arf! arf!—ring in the morning.'

They all nodded. It was a small community. They owed him a lot.

'Never steal beef, do they?' said an ex-shepherd, forced now to open a discotheque. 'What kind of rustlers steals only sheep?'

They were still deliberating upon this, when the bar-doors flew suddenly open, and a distraught and trail-stained farm-worker hurled himself among them. His eyes were wild, and his trembling finger jabbed behind him.

'Come quick!' he croaked, and ran out again.

The lawman rushed after him, pausing only to fix his clips, sharpen his pencil, adjust his chinstrap, tune his whistle, and telephone the greengrocer. Within minutes, he was riding after the vanishing dot.

He caught him on the outskirts of town. The man was hiding behind a tree and pointing across open country to a cloud of moving dust.

'Rustlers!' he cried, as the lawman dismounted and began oiling his chain. He put his ear to the ground.

'Not making much noise,' said the lawman. 'You'd expect the thunder of hooves.'

'Not with chickens,' said the farm-worker.

The lawman looked again, It was true. A vast herd of Leghorns was galloping into the distance. Dimly, through the rising dust, they could make out the figure of a man on a moped, waving an umbrella to urge them on.

'Come on!' cried the farmworker.

The lawman sucked his lip, thumb in his belt, eye on the sun. He put up a wet finger, testing the wind.

'We'd best be off home, now,' he said. 'You can't never tell with chickens. Get in among that lot, you'd be pecked to ribbons before you knew it. It'll all be in my report, after my elevenses.'

'Chickens now,' said his wife. 'First sheep, now chickens. No beef.' She wrung out the tea-bag and put it back in its jar. Times were hard. Dripping hardly stained the bread, these days. 'I know!' she said suddenly. 'It's someone selling to the Indians!'

The lawman went upstairs, not speaking, and had a bath. He came down again. It was nearly noon.

'There's a thought,' he said.

He knew Indians and Indian territory like the back of his hand. He had known it in the days when it was Ye Olde Kopper Kettle. He took his helmet off, and went in. His serge arm rasped on the flock wallpaper, and an Indian slid out of nowhere at the sound.

'I am saying good day to you, what incredibly magnificent weather we are having, my goodness,' said the lawman, who had studied their ways and knew their tongues. 'Is it possible for you to be telling me what it is you are offering on the Businessman's Special this fine day?'

'Lamb curry,' grunted the Indian, 'tandoori chicken, mutton Madras.'

'Would it be possible for you to be giving me the incredibly necessary information concerning where you are purchasing this meat, by Jove?' said the lawman.

'Bloke comes Wednesdays,' said the Indian. 'Does me first, then he's off down the OK Grill-Room, isn't he? Probably catch him there now, if you're quick.'

'It has been an indescribable pleasure talking to you, oh my word, yes,' said the lawman, and backed out, bowing.

The sun glared fierce in the street. It hung overhead, like a great brass gong. It was noon. There was no-one else about. He thought of getting the Doc, but this was the time he took his linctus. He thought of asking some of the other citizens, but he knew what their reaction would be. They'd tell him to do something.

He was about to tiptoe, with his slow, easy, loping tiptoe, past the OK Grill-Room, when the door opened, and a man came out. He wore a black jacket, waistcoat and striped trousers, and a bowler hat. In one hand he carried an umbrella, in the other a rifle. He looked at the lawman.

'Oh I say!' he said. 'Haw, haw, haw! Well I jolly old never! A jolly old harry coppers!'

The lawman looked at the gun, and he looked at the man, and his throat was dry. But a man had to do what a man had to do. The lawman jerked his head towards a Jaguar parked at the kerb. A sheep's head was sticking out of the boot, dripping on the pullets tied to the rear bumper.

'Is this your car?' said the lawman.

'Jolly old is, I'm afraid, haw, haw, haw!' said the man with the gun.

The lawman drew in his breath.

'Can't leave it there,' he said. 'That's a double yellow line.'

Owing to Circumstances Beyond our Control 1984 has been Unavoidably Detained . . .

in which I set out to prove that totalitarianism in Britain could never work. How could it, when nothing else does?

WINSTON SMITH lay on his mean little bed in his mean little room and stared at his mean little telescreen. The screen stared back, blank. Smith eased himself from the side of his mean little blonde, walked across his dun and threadbare carpet, and kicked the silent cathode. A blip lurched unsteadily across it, and disappeared. Smith sighed, and picked up the telephone.

'Would you get me Rentabrother Telehire?' he said.

'They're in the book,' said the operator.

'I haven't got a book,' said Smith. 'They didn't deliver it.'

'It's no good blaming me,' said the operator. 'It's a different department.'

'I'm not blaming you,' said Smith. 'I just thought you might get me the number.'

'I was just going off,' said the operator, 'on account of the snow.'

'It's not snowing,' said Smith.

'Not *now*, it isn't,' said the operator. 'I never said it was snowing *now*.'

'Perhaps I might have a word with the Supervisor,' said Smith.

'She's not here,' said the operator. 'She gets her hair done Fridays.'

'I only need the Rentabrother number,' said Smith, 'perhaps you could find it for me. You must have a book.'

'I'd have to bend,' said the operator.

124

'I'd be awfully grateful,' said Smith.

'I've just done me nails.'

'Please,' said Smith.

There was a long pause, during which a woman came on and began ordering chops, and someone gave Smith a snatch of weather forecast for Heligoland. After that, there was a bit of recipe for sausage toad. Eventually, after two further disconnections, the operator came back.

'It's 706544,' she snapped.

Smith put the receiver down, and dialled 706544.

'809113,' shouted a voice, 'Eastasian Cats Home.'

He got a Samoan ironmonger after that, and then a French woman who broke down and screamed. At last 'Rentabrother Telehire,' said a man.

'Winston Smith here,' said Smith, '72a, Osbaldeston Road. I'm afraid my telescreen seems to be out of order.'

'What am I supposed to do?' said the man. 'We're up to our necks.'

'But I'm not being watched,' said Smith. 'Big Brother is supposed to be monitoring me at all times.'

'Ring Big Bleeding Brother, then,' said the man. 'Maybe he's not suffering from staff shortages, seasonal holidays, people off sick. Maybe he's not awaiting deliveries. Not to mention we had a gull get in the stockroom, there's stuff all over, all the labels come off, broken glass. People ringing up all hours of the day and night. You realise this is my tea-time?'

'I'm terribly sorry,' said Smith, 'It's just that . . .'

'Might be able to fit you in Thursday fortnight,' said the man. 'Can't promise nothing, though. Got a screwdriver, have you?'

'I'm not sure,' said Smith.

'Expect bleeding miracles, people,' said the man, and rang off.

Smith put the phone down, and was about to return to the bed when there was a heavy knocking on the door, and before he or the little blonde could move, it burst from its hinges and two enormous constables of the Thought Police hurtled into the room. They recovered, and looked around, and took out notebooks.

'Eric Jervis', cried the larger of the two, 'we have been

monitoring your every action for the past six days, and we have reason to believe that the bicycle standing outside with the worn brake blocks is registered in your name. What have you to say?'

'I'm not Eric Jervis,' said Smith.

They stared at him.

'Here's a turn-up,' said the shorter officer.

'Ask him if he's got any means of identity,' murmured the larger.

'Have you any means of identity?' said the constable.

'I'm waiting for a new identity card,' said Smith. 'It's in the post.'

'I knew he'd say that,' said the larger officer.

'We're right in it now,' said his colleague. 'Think of the paperwork.'

They put their notebooks away.

'You wouldn't know where this Eric Jervis is, by any chance?' said the taller.

'I'm afraid not,' said Smith.

'Who's that on the bed, then?'

'It's certainly not Eric Jervis,' said Smith.

They all looked at the little blonde.

'He's got us there,' said the shorter constable.

'I've just had a thought,' said the taller, 'I don't think people are supposed to, er, do it, are they?'

'Do what?'

'You know, men,' the Thought Policeman looked at his boots, 'and women.'

'I don't see what that's got to do with worn brake blocks,' said his colleague.

They tipped their helmets.

'Mind how you go,' they said.

Smith let them out, and came back into the room.

'I'll just nip down the corner,' he said to the little blonde, 'and pick up an evening paper. Shan't be a tick.'

It was crowded on the street. It was actually the time of the two minutes hate, but half the public telescreens were conked out, and anyway the population was largely drunk, or arguing with one another, or smacking kids round the head, or running to get a bet on, or dragging dogs from lamp-posts, or otherwise

126

pre-occupied, so nobody paid much attention to the suspended telescreens, except for the youths throwing stones at them. Smith edged through, and bought a paper, and opened it.

'COME OFF IT BIG BROTHER!,' screamed the headline, above a story blaming the Government for rising food prices, the shortage of underwear, and the poor showing of the Oceanic football team. It wasn't, Smith knew, the story the Government hacks had given to the printers, but you could never get the printers to listen to anyone, and challenged, they always blamed the shortage of type, claiming that they could only put the words together from the letters available, and who cared, anyhow? The Government, with so much else on its plate, had given up bothering.

It was as Winston Smith turned to go back to his flat, that he felt a frantic plucking at his knee, and heard a soprano scream ring through the street. He looked down, and saw a tiny Youth Spy jumping up and down below him.

'Winston Smith does dirty things up in Fourteen B,' howled the child. 'Come and get him, he's got a nude lady up there.'

The youth spy might have elaborated on these themes, had its mother not reached out and given it a round arm swipe that sent it flying into the gutter: but, even so, the damage had been done, and before Smith had time to protest, he found himself picked up bodily by a brace of uniformed men and slung into the back of a truck which, siren wailing, bore him rapidly through the evening streets towards the fearful pile of the Ministry of Love.

'Smith, W,' barked the uniformed man to whom Smith was manacled, at the desk clerk.

'What's he done?' said the clerk. 'I was just off home.'

'They caught him at a bit of how's your father,' said Smith's captor.

'It's Friday night,' said the desk clerk. 'I go to bingo Fridays.' He turned to Smith. 'Don't let it happen again, lad. You can go blind.'

'I've written him in me book,' said the guard. 'It's no good saying go home. I'd have to tear the page out.' He put his free hand on Smith's arm. 'Sorry about this, son. It'd be different if I had a rubber. We're awaiting deliveries.'

'You'd better take him up to Room 101, then,' said the clerk.

'NOT ROOM 101,' screamed Smith, 'NOT THE TORTURE CHAM-
BER, PLEASE, I NEVER DID ANYTHING, I HARDLY KNOW THE
WOMAN, CAN'T ANYONE HELP ME, DON'T SEND ME UP . . .'

'Stop that,' said the clerk, sharply. 'You'll start the dog off.'

Smith was dragged, shrieking, to the lift.

'Ah, Smith, Winston,' cried the white-coated man at the
door of Room 101. 'Won't you come in? Rats I believe, are what
you, ha-ha-ha, fear most of all. Big brown rats. Big brown pink-
eyed rats . . .'

'NO,' screamed Smith, 'NOT RATS, ANYTHING BUT RATS, NO,
NO, NO.'

'. . . Rats with long slithery tails, Smith, fat, hungry rats, rats
with sharp little . . .'

'Oh, do shut up, Esmond,' interrupted his assistant wearily.
'You know we haven't got any rats. We haven't seen a rat since
last December's delivery.'

'No rats?' gasped Smith.

Esmond sighed, and shook his head. Then he suddenly
brightened.

'We've got mice though,' he cried. 'Big fat, hungry, pink-
eyed . . .'

'I don't mind mice,' said Smith.

They looked at him.

'You're not making our job any easier, you know,' muttered
Esmond.

'Try him on toads,' said Esmond's assistant. 'Can't move in
the stockroom for toads.'

'That's it!' exclaimed Esmond. 'Toads, Big, fat, slimy . . .'

'I quite like toads,' said Smith.

There was a long pause.

'Spiders?'

'Lovely little things,' said Smith. 'If it's any help, I can't
stand moths.'

'Moths,' cried Esmond. 'Where do you think you are, bloody
Harrod's? We can't get moths for love nor money.'

'Comes in here, big as you please, asking for moths,' said
Esmond's assistant.

Smith thought for a while.

'I'm not all that keen on stoats,' he said at last.

'At last,' said Esmond. 'I thought we'd be here all night. Give him a stoat, Dennis.'

So they put Winston Smith in Room 101 with a stoat. It was an old stoat, and it just sat on the floor, wheezing, and as far as Smith was concerned, things could have been, all things considered, a lot worse.

God Help Us for We Knew the Worst Too Young

News that flying truancy squads have been set up by a number of police forces to catch absentee kids leads me to wonder where it will all go from there

'PRISONER AT THE BAR, you are charged that on the afternoon of February 10, 1975, you did absent yourself without authority from Foskett Road Junior School, that when apprehended upon the premises of the Ram Gopal Fish and Takeaway Tandoori Parlour you told a whopping great fib, and that you were subsequently found to have in your possession a number of forged documents, to whit, a note ostensibly signed by your mother explaining that you were suffering from a bilious attack, a letter purporting to come from your doctor excusing you from school on the grounds that you had contracted bubonic plague from your cat, and a telegram signed by the Queen saying that it was a Muslim holiday. How do you plead?'

'Not guilty,' said a voice from a space between two policemen.

The judge leaned forward.

'Do you think,' he murmured, 'we could get him a box to stand on?'

A box having been brought, a small head appeared on the rim of the dock, and the counsel for the prosecution rose once more to his feet.

'Call Inspector Finch,' he said.

The court held its breath.

'I swear by Almighty God,' said the Inspector, 'that the evidence I shall. . . .'

The judge leaned forward again.

'I think, perhaps,' he murmured, 'another box might be in order?'

After a minute or two, the Inspector's head emerged above the witness-box.

'. . . shall give shall be the truth, the whole truth, and nothing but the truth. Inspector Charles Finch, Truancy Squad, Q Division.'

The judge looked at him.

'I trust you will not take this as an intrusion, Inspector,' he said, 'but you appear to be considerably less than five feet tall.'

'Not considerably, m'lud,' said the Inspector. 'I would not say considerably. Marginally would be more the term I would select.'

The judge wrote something on his pad, carefully.

'If I might enlighten the court, my lord,' said the prosecuting counsel, 'there is no officer in the Truancy Squad above five feet in height. They are specially selected, my lord. Working as they do in plain clothes, under cover, as it were, mingling unnoticed with those base elements in our society which it is their duty to apprehend, it will readily be appreciated that the appropriate stature is of the utmost importance. A six-foot boy in a cap and short trousers might arouse suspicion, do you see?'

The judge nodded.

'He would dwarf his pencil-box,' he said. 'His, er, cover would be instantly, um, blown, I believe the word is, ha-ha-ha!'

'Ha-ha-ha!' shrieked the prosecuting counsel astutely. 'My lord tempers, as ever, wisdom and understanding with wonderful wit!'

'Toady!' cried the counsel for the defence, springing to his feet. 'Crawler! Judge's pet!'

'SILENCE!' roared the judge. He pushed his bi-focals down his nose and stared at the defence counsel, most of whose head was enveloped in his wig, and whose gown covered his hands completely, and trailed on the floor. 'Am I to take it,' said the judge, 'that defence counsel in this case is also, begging the inspector's pardon, a midget?'

The prosecuting counsel cleared his throat.

'The prisoner, my lord,' he said, 'is represented by his friend Douglas. It is, as you I'm sure know, quite in order. *McKenzie's Friend*, my lord.'

'It is not in order for him to wear a wig,' replied the judge, 'if he is not a member of the Bar.'

'An attempt was made to remove the item from him, m'lud,' said the Clerk, 'but he bit us.'

'Serves you right!' shouted the defence counsel.

'Is counsel for the defence eating?' cried the judge.

'What if I am?'

'COME OUT HERE!' shouted the judge.

The counsel for the defence groped across the floor of the court, like a wounded bat, and put his boiled sweet on the edge of the judge's table. He paused on his returning shuffle, before the Clerk's bench.

'I want a receipt for that,' he said.

'May I continue, my lord?' said the prosecuting counsel. He turned to the tiny face of the Inspector. 'Do go on.'

The policeman flipped open his notebook.

'On the afternoon of February 10, 1975,' he said, 'I was on patrol, cruising along the pavement of Holloway Road, when I observed the prisoner through the window of the Ram Gopal Fish and Takeaway Tandoori Parlour. I parked my tricycle and approached. He was eating a piece of skate, and his side pocket contained what was clearly a folded school cap.'

'SNEAK!' cried the counsel for the defence.

'Approach the bench at once!' snapped the judge. He leaned forward, and smacked the defence counsel across the wig. 'One more interruption, and you will stay behind after court. Go on, Inspector.'

'I entered the establishment and engaged the prisoner in a conversation about Biffo the Bear to lull his suspicions.'

The judge held up his hand and looked at the Clerk.

'This, er, Bingo the, er. . . .'

'Biffo, m'lud,' said the Clerk. 'He is a fictional animal.'

'A sort of Ego the Ostrich, you mean?' said the judge.

'Exactly, m'lud.'

The Inspector cleared his throat behind a tiny, delicate hand.

'It was in the subsequent course of this conversation, that I was able to ascertain that the prisoner should at that moment have been doing tens and units with Miss Perrins at Foskett Road Junior School. I produced my warrant card and advised him of his rights.'

'What did the prisoner say?' asked the prosecuting counsel.

'He said I,' the Inspector held his book to the light and squinted at it, '. . . said I had a face like a dog's bum and he would get his gang on me and bash me up.'

The court gasped! A Chief Superintendent went pale! A jurywoman reached for the rail, and held on bravely!

'This gang,' muttered the judge, 'you know of them?'

'Oh, yes, my lord,' said the Inspector. 'They are known as the Black Daleks. They meet in a shed and have a special handshake and wear their caps backwards. It is rumoured that they bake their conkers, among other things, also put newts in girls' knickers, not to mention. . . .'

'OBJECTION!' cried the counsel for the defence.

'Yes?' said the judge.

'No we never,' said the counsel for the defence. 'He is thinking of worms.'

'Overruled,' said the judge.

'He then produced Exhibit A, claiming that it was from his mother. The court will observe that "bilious" has been spelt with three l's. When I told the prisoner that this was not satisfactory, he showed me the letter from his doctor, which contained the information that bubonic plague can only be cured by eating skate. Exhibit C, my lord, merely reads: ALL YOU MUSLIMS CAN HAVE NEXT WEEK OFF SIGNED YOUR MAJESTY THE QUEEN.'

'I have no further questions, m'lud,' said the prosecuting counsel.

The counsel for the defence stood up, imperceptibly.

'Inspector Finch,' he said, somewhat muffled through the enfolding wig, 'are you or are you not a being from outer space, probably Jupiter?'

'No.'

'There you are then!' cried the wig triumphantly. '*The very last thing a being from outer space come here to bear off our women on account of there has been a nuclear holocaust on Jupiter and their women have all turned into loony maneating jellyfish and the race is in danger of dying out would do is admit it!*' He sat down again. 'No further questions.'

The prosecuting counsel rose.

'That is the case for the prosecution, my lord,' he said.

'I call the prisoner,' said the defence counsel.

The prisoner crossed to the witness box, and took the oath.

'Would you tell the court, in your own words,' said his counsel, 'exactly what your secret mission is?'

'Yes,' said the prisoner, 'provided they keep shut up about it. I think they ought to know I can kill people with a single Look.'

The judge took off his spectacles.

'What kind of look?' he said.

'I am not at liberty to divulge that, m'lud,' said the prisoner. 'But if you got it, you'd know.' He glanced about him, darkly. 'On the day in question, I was on a secret mission to stop the earth getting invaded by beings from outer space. There is a lot of this about, as everybody knows. I was sitting in the window of the fish shop disguised as an ordinary person eating skate, but really I was keeping watch for anything with nine legs, or green, or blatting anyone with their gamma guns, that sort of thing. It was while I was doing this that a midget came up to me, disguised as a boy, and began talking about Biffo the Bear.'

'How did you know,' asked the defence counsel, 'that he was a midget?'

'He had hair in his nostrils, and when you looked close you could see he had little tiny whiskers all over his face. We are trained,' and here the prisoner turned to the rapt jury, 'to notice these things. Also, any fool knows that Biffo the Bear has not been in the *Beano* for some years. It was just like when they drop Russian agents in places and the Russian agents go *What-ho, top-hole, jolly good, by Jove* and all that stuff, and you know they are really people called Ivan who've been mugging up Billy Bunter or somebody. Luckily, I had with me my Special Documents. . . .'

'Exhibits A, B, and C, my lord,' said his counsel.

'. . . because the one thing beings from outer space are scared of is catching alien bacteria, as everybody knows, such as a bilious attack or bubonic plague or something Muslim.'

'You may step down,' said his counsel.

'No questions,' said the prosecution, wearily.

Whereupon, the summings-up having been eschewed, the jury filed out, filed back a minute or two later, and without a second's pause declared the prisoner Not Guilty.

Which, in view of the fact that they were twelve honest, stout, upstanding British citizens who had all previously written notes explaining that they would be unable to do jury service because of bilious attacks, nosebleeds, dying relatives, flat feet, indispensability at work, snow on the points, old war wounds and religious holidays, all of which had been refused point blank by the Sheriff, was hardly surprising.

Every Cloud has a Nickel Lining

Apartment 3b
Walnut Street
Orange, N.J.

DEAR MR. HEFNER:

I read just now where the Playboy organisation is feeling the, you know, economic pinch and where you are cutting back on unnecessary expenditure e.g. grounding Big Bunny, making people turn off lights, reducing expense accounts, stopping free executive coffee and so forth, and while I, like, sympathise with your plight, I have to say that this development is very exciting to people such as me.

For many years now, I have been a devoted reader of your wonderful magazine which seems to me to sum up what the American dream is all about, also have collected one of the most impressive collections on our block of your wonderful Playboy gift opportunities, and I do not think a month goes by without my sending up for one of your chance-of-a-lifetime offers such as the outstanding simulated-goldette cufflinks with the rabbits on and the fairly-luminous key-ring and the smart tie where the rabbit looks like it's real when you breathe in and out, especially with the bunny tie-clip, it has this practically genuine rhinestone eye which follows you round the room and makes the middle of your shirt a thrilling conversation piece for young and old.

I also have a number of marvellous real plastic swizzle-sticks that I have made into a mobile for my room, you would think you were in a sheek penthouse, all these little rabbits in the air everywhere, plus pictures taken from a decade of gatefolds stuck up round my walls, they could be real women, I mean, you'd think I was entertaining these fantastic nude ladies if you, like, just glanced at them quickly as you walked in, or were very short-sighted such as me.

I also have a special offer ice-tray which makes ice in the shape of, er, boobs and when they clink against the side of this very smart glass I have with most of the thrilling three-colour transfer left on it, you would think you were in El Morocco or somewhere, instead of being on your own three flights up in Orange, New Jersey, above the Sam Pinchus Takeaway Pastrami Lounge.

And not only do I have all this wonderful range of executive items around me all the time, enriching my life etcetera, I have also taken your marvellous expert advice in the matter of drinking, smoking, male cosmetics and similar: many an unforgettable evening have I spent, swivelling in my mouth-watering Mister Executive chair, a long glass of tequila 'n' chicken broth in my fist, an imperial-size cherry menthol stogie in my mouth, and my whole body giving off the soft odour of smouldering tumbleweed aftershave, as I chat nonchalantly with Miss September 1968, who has been gummed to my door for six years now and knows more about me than my mother, or listen to the swinging brass of Herb Alpert on the half of the terrific-value seventy-dollar stereo kit I have been able to afford so far.

I see that I have touched on the subject of money, Mr. Hefner—or may I call you Hef? I have nearly saved up enough to buy a key for the New York Playboy Club Special Introductory Offer, and feel that as a fellow-member, well practically, I am on, you know, first-name terms with you—and that is really what I am writing to you about today. You see while I am working towards being a playboy, and have been these twelve years past, what with inflation and sending a bit to my mother and all I cannot altogether escape the feeling that it is taking me one hell of a time. I mean, I have the cufflinks and the glass and the eye-catching mock-onyxette desk set, which I forgot to mention earlier, and so forth, but there is no way of escaping the fact that my room is not a ten-thousand-square-foot penthouse overlooking the San Francisco Bay, especially when Sam Pinchus is cooking his two-dollar Lithuanian Special and you can smell the fried knackwurst on the *roof*, for Chrissake, which is where I go to get a rich golden tan, except I don't on account of the smog, what I do get is sooty specks from the Hackman Rolling Mills opposite, also, sometimes, a poke in the eye from Kowalski the janitor who has some crazy idea I'm going to touch his goddam pigeons.

I realise a playboy, with all that weight-training and rowing-machine and squash-playing stuff at the New York Athletic Club, should not take no lip from a lousy Polish janitor, but working overtime every night at the supermarket writing out labels so's I can afford all my wonderful interesting executive purchases, I do not get much exercise, also I am only five-feet-three-and-a-half, even in my Tallguy Special sixty-dollar elevated shoes. As a matter of fact, I once tried to kick Kowalski with these after he asked one of his stinking pigeons who the midget with the two club feet was, and if I had caught him I would have killed him on account of these shoes must weigh around eight pounds each, but it flew off and went over the edge of the roof, and I had to limp downstairs to get it before the dogs did (we have a lot of stray Dobermanns in this neighbourhood, God knows why), and I was unfortunate enough to bump into Miss Natalie Birnbaum, whom I am hoping to make when I am a full member of the club, and I think it set back my chances more than somewhat when Miss Birnbaum saw that half of me was only four-feet-eleven-and-a-quarter.

Do not think that Miss Natalie Birnbaum is any, you know, Playmate Of The Month, Hef. She is 31-30-38, at a guess, and will not see forty again, but with the light behind her you would not guess she has a moustache, and, which is the main thing, she lives in Apartment 2c, and is the only girl I know.

One day I will take her out in my threetone 1959 Volkswagen with the terrific yellow wing and the nearly-whole fenders, if I can ever afford the two re-treads for the back, and we shall drive to the top of somewhere not too steep, and I shall put a brick under the rear wheels and get back inside and when the moon comes up over New Jersey, I shall grab her and try to undo her bra again, the way I tried on November 18, 1967.

I would like, of course, to lean nonchalantly on her door-jamb and invite her to weekend with me in Nassau, where we would drink out of my Playboy glass and admire my cufflinks and tie-clip before getting onto the round bed in the Scheherezade Suite of the Playboy Hotel, but as the best I can do at present is a Greyhound ticket to Newark, I shall have to shelve that for a while.

You may think I have wandered from my drift, Hef, but may

I assure you to the contrary, and thank you, by the way, for helping me to increase my vocabulary so superbly over the years? My drift is that if things are really looking a bit grim at *Playboy*, if you're going in for, like, economies and cutbacks and all, it could be that things are turning my way at long last, especially with the dollar not looking too good no more and everyone nipping and tucking and looking around for what they can save on. I mean it could be, couldn't it, that one day you're gonna find that shelling out ten thousand large ones for Miss August or whatever isn't on, and—well, I mean, I know you won't get no Natalie Birnbaum, but it's possible the gatefold will droop a little, squint a little, have maybe a wart or two, even a little acne, right? Also, you'll be giving a bit less coverage to three-month private yacht cruises in the Mediterranean Ocean, more to—okay, not Newark, but Atlantic City, possibly? And instead of pushing the Ferrari Dino or the, you know, Mercedes C-111, it's gonna be the new Chevrolet compact, where the guy—let's say he's five-eight, going a little thin—not bald, but thin—on top, with maybe a crease or two in his suit and some of the simulated-goldette rubbing off his cufflinks, takes this girl with the wart and the fat ankles, but a really nice smile and quite a few good teeth in it, out for a meal at—not Sam Pinchus's, I don't ask that—the Pompadour Eating Parlour of the Milton Hotel, Jersey City, where they have a $5.95 platter including four guaranteed butterfly prawns, you'd think you were in Paris, France.

I would like it very much if things turned out that way, Hef. I'm thirty-eight next March, and I look very much like being thirty-nine the March after that. I am quite prepared to go on dreaming, Hef, I have never been a quitter, but I am getting to the stage where it would sure help if you could see your way clear to fixing things so's the dream met me half-way.

> Your devoted reader and friend,
> *Arthur L. Farfel Jr.*

It is Backs to the Wall, My Kinsmen, it is Backs to the Wall Again!

The Association of County Councils has warned that unless ways are quickly found of raising 'hundreds of millions of pounds', local government services will be drastically cut back.

THE MEETING OF THURSDAY, December 18, came to order.

Councillor Mrs. Belwether thanked the Council for their courtesy in deferring the commencement of proceedings and apologised for her lateness. She explained that she had been assisting a dustman in carrying her bins to the cart. She had watched him from her window and grown curious as to why he was carrying one jam jar at a time and walking into the fence. On being approached, he informed her that he had been disorientated since the retreat from Mons. On that occasion he had ended up in Denmark.

Councillor Garmole said that he did not see where the jam jar came in.

Councillor Mrs. Belwether explained that she had been informed by the dustman that the highest medical opinion had forbidden him to carry anything heavy following his contraction of a hernia during an Abdication party.

Councillor Jerrold said that was all very well, but the main business of the day was to give attention to alleviating those conditions that had resulted in the city being served by octogenarian dustmen, and had everyone seen his memorandum of the sixteenth inst. regarding millionaire oil sheikhs.

Councillor Mrs. J. Soames said that she had perused it at length but was unable to see what might attract millionaire oil sheikhs to their midst.

Councillor Jerrold asked her to forgive his astonishment, but

140

had it escaped her attention that millionaire oil sheikhs were always coming over here and having major heart surgery which they could not obtain for love nor money on the Persian Gulf?

Councillor Mrs. J. Soames said that to her certain knowledge there was no major heart surgeon in the borough and the only thing they did up the cottage hospital was lance boils and similar, and you wouldn't get people jetting in from Kuwait to have a carbuncle felt.

Councillor Jerrold said that she seemed to be forgetting the slipper baths. In his travels to many parts of the globe, he maintained, he had seen none better. There was nothing an oil sheikh liked more, he said, than lying back and having a good towelling. He had seen many films where this had happened.

Councillor Garmole said you needed eunuchs for that kind of thing.

Councillor Jerrold said that Councillor Garmole was always raising piddling bleeding objections. He asked the Council to pardon his French. He said that nobody could say with any certainty how many eunuchs there were in the borough, it was not the sort of thing people went round admitting. You would have to advertise, in a nice way.

Councillor Mrs. Belwether said that she did not like the turn the meeting was taking. She said that she also intended to raise at another time and in a higher place the suggestion in Councillor Jerrold's memorandum concerning the sale of virgins.

Councillor Foskett arrived and apologised for being late. He explained that he had stopped to aid a lollipop man who had fallen over on his crossing. The man had pointed out that he had not been able to stand up for any length of time since the retreat from Mons. He had also been deeply upset that morning when a dustcart had run away from him and demolished the slipper baths.

Councillor Jerrold asked Councillor Foskett to repeat what he had just said.

Councillor Foskett did so.

Councillor Jerrold said that everything now depended upon the Borough Museum's collection of Victorian photographs. He drew the attention of the Council to that paragraph in his memorandum which pointed out how millions of American visitors would be fascinated to see how the High Street had changed since 1879. He anticipated that sales of commemorative ashtrays and humorous wallets alone would be more than enough to maintain the street lighting to the highest standards.

Councillor Mrs. J. Soames said that she did not think the High Street had changed much since 1879.

Councillor Jerrold said that she did not understand the Americans and their unceasing quest for knowledge. In the course of his travels to many parts of the globe, he had been to Stratford-upon-Avon and seen them buying historical tea-towels he would not give you a thank-you for.

Councillor Garmole was of the opinion that the High Street of Stratford-upon-Avon must have changed a damned sight more than theirs had. That was all he could say.

Councillor Foskett said that he was something of a philosopher and as such it appeared to him to be a shocking indictment that they could afford to send people to the Moon all right but there wasn't enough money to stop the sewage piling up. He wanted to know where it would all end.

Councillor Mrs. Belwether said that it was news to her that the Council had sent anyone to the Moon.

Councillor R. Beddoes said that he had maintained a watching brief up until that moment in time but that the hour had come for men of honour to break silence, especially when they had responsibility for sewage affairs and people started getting at them. He intended no slur to any previous speaker, but some people he could mention ought to watch themselves when they knew bugger-all whereof they spoke. The question of the sewage was, as they all knew full well, a question of undermanning. You could not expect a man who had been shot to bits at Mons to be everywhere at once. He took leave to wonder whether a certain Councillor not a million miles from that very spot would feel like running a sewage works at the age of eighty, it was hardly surprising the Hygiene Department fell down on its crossing.

Councillor Foskett said that he never said the Council had sent anyone to the Moon. If they wanted his honest opinion, he continued, the Borough ought to go bankrupt. His brother-in-law had gone bankrupt and now ran a very successful chain of coin-operated launderettes in the Algarve.

Councillor Garmole said that he failed to see how they could operate effectively from the Algarve. There was the language problem for a start. You could not run a borough from a thousand miles away.

Councillor Mrs. J. Soames said that the Estonian Government-in-Exile had not been back to Estonia since 1938.

Councillor Jerrold said O his God.

Councillor Mrs. J. Soames asked whether somebody had said something.

Councillor Jerrold said he merely wished to refer the Council once again to his memorandum. He wished to know why there had been no feedback from his suggestion that the next Olympic Games be held in the Borough. In the course of his travels to many parts of the globe, he had seen how Wembley had been transformed by the 1948 Games. People there, to his certain knowledge, had retired on fortunes made out of cheap cushions, model guardsmen with cigarettes in their busbies, commemorative trays, and the like. They would also end up with an international-standard swimming-pool, which could double as a slipper baths, as things had turned out. The Olympic Games would put the Borough on the map.

Councillor Garmole said the 1980 Olympic Games were going to be held in Moscow.

Councillor Jerrold said there he went again with his bloody niggling objections. 1980 was six years away, and anything could happen in six years. If people knew that the Olympic Games might be held in the Borough, support would flood in. It was only eighty minutes from Euston, for one thing, and everyone spoke English. He asked whether Moscow could say the same.

Councillor Foskett said that if they wanted his honest opinion, the Borough ought to go public. His cousin had gone public, and now lived in Nassau with a former novelty dancer.

Councillor Mrs. Belwether suggested that it seemed to be a good moment to adjourn for lunch. She begged leave to ring for the Catering Officer to enquire whether the meal was ready.

The Catering Officer appeared after some minutes and explained that he would be unable to prepare lunch, as he had to go off and paint a dotted line down the middle of the High Street. He said that the Council might be interested to learn that it was sixty years to the day since the last occasion on which he had worked his way backwards in the service of his country. He hoped, he said, that he would not end up in Denmark this time.

The meeting was adjourned.

One of Our Inputs is Missing

'Allegations about Value Added Tax officers carrying out Gestapo-like raids have highlighted the extraordinary powers available to low-grade civil servants to enforce the collection of VAT. Fears about these powers were first expressed nearly three years ago by the Law Society and the Bar Council. They warned, unavailingly, that the powers were frightening and unEnglish.' – The Observer

IN THE DARK ATTIC, the morse-key ticked its tinny chatter.

Nobody used the telephone any more.

'S-O-S, Charlie Dog,' the operator tapped laboriously. The sweat beading his thumb and forefinger slid evilly between desire and execution.

'Identify, Pharlie Fig,' bleeped his headphone.

The operator licked his lips, swallowed, blinked the droplets from his eyes.

'C-h-a-r-l-i-e D-o-g,' he tapped carefully. 'Reason — to — believe — they — are — on — to — me — have — failed — to — distinguish — between — partly — deductible — input — tax — under — Method — Two — and — wholly — deductible — input — tax — using — Method — One — and — cannot — now — divide — contents — of — Box — 14 — multiplied — by — one — hundred — by — contents — of — Box — 16 — and — multiply — same — by — 22 — Mayday — for — Gods — sake — or —"

'HA! WAS HAT MAN HIER GEFUNDEN?'

The operator spun around in the echo of splintered wood! There, framed in the ruined doorway, they stood, jackbooted legs apart, thigh muscles distorting the pinstriped lines to ovoids, the candle's pale highlights glinting off their iron bowlers.

145

They goosestepped into the little room, both of them, Lügers in one hand, calculators in the other, and stood either side of his chair.

The taller of the two brought his heels together and nodded the monocle from his terrible eye.

'So!' he barked. He paused and smiled a fearful smile, 'Gut evening, 230 7456 79, ve trust ve you in zer, how you say, pink of zer condition find?'

The operator said nothing.

The second officer wrenched the earphones from the operator's head.

'He is viz his liddle toy playing, Herr Oberst,' he murmured. 'He is perhaps a radio hem, ha-ha-ha!'

The first officer brought his gloved fist down on the tiny transmitter.

'It is a crystal set, Schulz,' he said. 'I believe cat's pyjamas is zer idiomatic name, is it not, 230 7456 79?'

'Whisker,' muttered the operator.

They looked at him.

'He talks in riddles, Schulz,' said the first officer.

'Und yet,' said Schulz, 'he claims that he such zimple items as zer walue of securities wizzin zer definition in zection 42 of zer Exchange Gontrol Ect 1947 it impossible to understand finds!'

'Neverzerless,' and here the first officer smiled his crooked smile once more, 've haf ways of making him . . .'

'Don't say it again,' said Schulz wearily, 'bitte.'

Whereupon each took hold of one of the operator's ears, and dragged him out.

They lay in the freezing grass, the moonlight winking off their frosted clothes.

They were just ordinary men, an antique dealer, two grocers, a family butcher, and a journalist. The journalist was something of an anomaly (he had always been) in that he had been both exempt *and* zero-rated in his time, but nobody would ever explain to him which he ought to be at any given moment, with the result that men kept coming round and distraining upon his chattels, just to make sure the law was not being made an ass. In consequence, the journalist now owned nothing but the suit

146

he stood up, or rather lay down, in.

'I hope to God they see our markers,' hissed the antique dealer.

The butcher sighed bitterly.

'We should have got in touch with them earlier,' he murmured. 'We were insane to try to go it alone, to take the swine on single-handed, without proper equipment, training, experience.'

'Amateurs,' muttered a grocer, 'against professionals!'

'And *crack* professionals,' said the other grocer. 'None of your Inland Revenue rubbish, none of . . .'

'Sssh!' hissed the journalist, cocking a blue ear.

There was no mistaking the throbby drone of the Dakota. It overflew the huddled rebels once, twice, then, blackening the moon, came lower and set down its human cargo.

The four hand-picked accountants loped across the meadow, crouching, and threw themselves down beside the waiting figures.

'Wisley, Wisley, Grunnett, and Wisley,' they whispered, severally.

'GUT EVENING, CHENTLEMEN!'

The spandaus cut down two of the Wisleys before they were half-way back to the plane. Grunnett, whose briefing had been necessarily short, ran around in total shrieking disorientation for a few seconds, before stepping on a mine.

And the third Wisley, who being the junior partner was somewhat fleeter of foot than the rest, covered all of two hundred yards, before the alsatians got him.

'How did the swine get onto us?' muttered the antique dealer, as they hurled him into the back of the truck.

The Obersturmbannführer turned in his seat, the smile gritted to the far end of his ivory cigarette-holder.

'Zer signal bonfire was you away giving!' he spat.

'Our bonfire?' said the butcher.

The Obersturmbannführer leaned over and stubbed his cigarette out in the butcher's ear.

'My men,' he said, 'are trained a burning ledger from fünf miles away to smell!'

'Welcome to Coldvatz,' said the Senior British Bankrupt.

'Thank you,' said the family butcher, the two grocers, the antique dealer, and the journalist.

'Most of the chaps here,' said the SBB, 'have come from other camps. I myself escaped twice from Stalag Vat III. I'm afraid this place is a somewhat tougher nut to crack.' He walked to the window of his little cell, and jabbed his swagger-stick at the scene beneath: the courtyard was full of steel desks, at which the guards sat in pairs, two guards to a comptometer and a stack of leather-bound books beside each one.

The Senior British Bankrupt clenched his jaw, and the muscles bunched along his temples.

'There isn't a loophole those johnnies can't plug,' he cried. 'Not a dodge, not a loose paragraph, not an ambiguous subsection the buggers aren't up to!'

'You have an Escape Officer, of course?' said the journalist.

'Did,' the SBB shook his elegant head, 'until yesterday. Doing fourteen years in solitary, now. He was working on an escape clause—Section 9, Paragraph 16, as a matter of fact, which exempts children's dresses from VAT. He was a gown manufacturer in civvy street, you know. Well, the goons found him working on a rebate claim form to the effect that what he had been engaged upon was the manufacture of clothes for giant children.'

'Bloody good!' cried the family butcher. 'Sounds watertight to me.'

The Senior British Bankrupt smiled a grim little smile.

'Easy to see you're a new boy,' he said. 'Not only did the Boche rush a White Paper out clarifying the thing before our chap's ink was dry, they also pulled in every school outfitter in the country on the grounds that *they* were evading tax on haberdashery for midgets. I have, naturally, complained to the Kommandant, but I very much . . .'

'. . . seems a perfectly reasonable appeal to me, Moan,' said the Kommandant. 'At zer time of his arrest, zis man predominantly in gymslips and blue knickers was, nicht wahr?'

'Gymslips!' shrieked Major Moan, his livid scars flushing like neons, 'Knickers! Herr Kommandant, vis respect, you are in zer past living! You are back to zer bad old days of zer old regime constantly harking! It is vis you Internalrevenuemacht

148

people always zer same, you care for nussing but zer correct coding! For years you zer setting-up of bogus companies villy-nilly allowed haf, zer making of wives into directors, nicht wahr, zer allowance against tax of veekend cottidges, modor-cars, holidays, tee-wee rental, telephones, dinner yackets, entertaining foreign buyers—YOU HAF ZER SWINE EVERY POSSIBLE DEDUCTION ALLOWED!'

He stopped in mid-stride, panting, pulling his rumpled jacket back beneath his gleaming Sam Browne.

'I am still,' said the Kommandant, 'zer Kommandant.'

Major Moan glanced sideways at him.

'You are forgetting why I in zis situation put been haf,' he said, quietly. 'You are failing to recognise zer position of zer Reichskanzler's chosen Customs und Excise Diwision, my friend.'

'I know you in high places friends haf,' said the Kommandant, 'but . . .'

'It so heppens,' murmured Moan, 'I only two days ago at a private luncheon vis Reichskanzler Healey talking was. *Ve are them by zer shorts und curlies grasping, Herr Major*, he told me from his position at zer top of zer curtains, *ve are* SOAKING *them!*'

Moan strode suddenly to the huge wall-map, cracked his whip-butt against it.

'Wictory is vizzin our grasp, Kommandant!' he cried. 'Trapped between zer Inlandrevenuemacht und zer Kapital-gainskommando to zer left, und zer Transfertax SS und Deaths Duty Battalion to zer right, what can they do but back against our crack VAT brigades fall? Und so, close we zer pincer, ja?'

The old Kommandant looked into Moan's burning eyes, and had to look away again. These young men, he thought, these young men. He shrugged.

'Heil Healey,' he muttered.

'I have received a postcard,' shouted the Senior British Bank-rupt, his breath pluming the icy air, 'from, er, Uncle Charlie!'

'HURRAH!' roared the assembled prisoners, the echo clatter-ing off the courtyard's ancient stones.

'He says he had a lovely journey and he sends a special kiss to all his old nephews in Compound Twelve. And if any of you wants to contact him, he can be reached c/o Account Number

5607893/45b, Bank of Zurich! The card is postmarked,' and here the SBB waved it above his head, 'Switzerland!'

The cheering went on for fifteen minutes. He had made it! Old Charlie had made it! And if he had made it, then . . .

They went back happily to their huts, to dream.

A Slight Attack of Jaundice

In which I crave the reader's indulgence

I ENJOYED TYPING 'crave the reader's indulgence' just now. I like old phrases, yesteryear's clichés; apart from being the only antiques I can afford, they offer a duckboard across the slime of linguistic ephemera in which the incautious journalist may find himself being sucked down for the third time. They are also a link, however rubbed and worn with use, across the scribbling eons; I touch writers long dead with such phrases. I am often, for example, tempted to start articles with 'I take up my pen in this year of grace 19—'; but nobody lets me, much.

(*'He's in a bloody peculiar mood this week,'* said the Reader, *'he isn't half going on.'* The Reader's wife turned up *'The Pallisers'* a decibel. *'What does he want this time?'* she shouted. *'He's craving my indulgence,'* said the Reader. *'Silly sod,'* said his wife.)

On this occasion, however, the phrase is more than mere decor. Indulgence is just exactly what I require, and if I have to crave to get it, then crave I shall. For I wish to grab someone by the lapel, and unburden what may well be my soul; and my wife is busy right now, and I do not have an analyst, and the barman in our local estaminet does not go in for pastoral care, it's as much as you can do to catch his eye for a small Worthington, and although the slogan 'That's what friends are for' enjoys some currency, it is not the way friends see it, I find.

Which leaves you.

I cannot be certain what has brought on my curious state of mind. I cannot, in fact, be certain what that state of mind is. It is not gloom, nor pessimism, though it seems tinted with both, and it is not fear, though fear is there in its seasoning. You might, I suppose, call it a sort of wry despair. I am locked, in

short, into a view of the Human Condition, and while I appreciate that this sort of entrapment should have been shogged off
with adolescence, when a melting ice-cream betokened morta-
lity and all that, I can only say that I still get it in infrequent re-
current bouts, like malaria, and there is little I can do but sweat
it out until the fever breaks, gripping the nearest hand. Yours.

Who can tell why it has struck today? The aftermath of that
preposterous election, perhaps, with its mock heroic stature, its
burlesque of destiny's crossroads, all those Gilbert and Sullivan
returning officers and candidates' wives in eau-de-nil suits?
The Irish burning their jails down, then huddling in the sleet
warming their hands on the embers of Nissen Block Fourteen?
The pathetic fallacy of thunder in October, could it be? Weird
weather ever did strange things to men. It cocks up the brain's
delicate electro-chemistry, I understand, not to mention turning cream and salmon.

Anyway, whatever its provenance, the disease has struck,
and what it means is that wherever I look, I find only lunacy
and disorder. Let us take the case of Dickie and Dottie.

Dickie and Dottie, you will remember, are the stage names of
Richard and Dorothy Arnold, and the most recent stage upon
which they were employed was in a room above the Pig and
Whistle in Dublin, as a result of which Dickie and Dottie found
themselves in court on four charges of indecency. Dottie, it was
alleged, had gone through a form of marriage with a cham-
pagne bottle, and Dickie was said to have used a large pair of
rubber hands to scratch his genitals during the show. 'That sort
of thing might go down well in the North of England,' said the
judge, 'but not in Dublin.' 'I have been an enormous success in
Baghdad and Beirut,' said Dickie, or was it Dottie, 'and next
month we are off on a tour of Israel.'

Was I alone, I wonder, in having a mind's eye that saw the
wonderful couple finding, at last, a room in Bethlehem to lay
their heads; and, just prior to lowering their limbs into the
humble straw, unpacking their giant rubber hands and bottle?
The star you can see in the east, by the way, in the top left-hand
corner of my mind's eye and just above Dottie's G-string, is a
Syrian 105-millimetre shell going off.

On the same day, at Luton, the case came up of the Special
Branch detective who was on duty at Luton Airport when he

was offered a free flight to Lourdes with a planeload of pilgrims. 'The party,' reported the *Daily Telegraph*, 'began drinking at the airport, had more drink during the flight to France, carried on drinking at Tarbes, the French airport, and drank during the return flight to Luton.' One of the upshots of which is that the Special Branch detective is now an ex-Special Branch detective, as a result of making a pass at one of the pilgrim's wives and having the pilgrim in question take a swing at him.

Why does this depress me? Normally, the thought of a stratosphere full of drunk pilgrims groping one another's spouses, maidservants, oxen and asses as they hurtled towards some sacred rendezvous would elicit no more than a shrug at the Way Of The World. I suppose it is when one takes such items in conjunction with others that the spirit begins to sag. Again, upon that very same day, the House of Lords decided that a colour bar was legal in the Dockers' Labour Club of Preston. And as if that alone were not enough—

'There's nothing personal in this,' said a member of the club responsible for instigating the ban, 'I have known the coloured gentleman in question for many years.'

With friends like that, who. . . .?

Let us remove Preston, briefly, from the hook. Let us expand our horizons from the narrow domestic view, and take in that cemetery in Buenos Aires from which, last week, the decayed remains of General Pedro Aramburu were stolen by a group ol Montoneros, an urban guerrilla army, who said the corpse was not fit to lie beside that of President Peron. As they were the ones who murdered Aramburu in the first place, four years ago, who am I to argue?

Should I draw your attention to the remarks of the South African Minister of Information, Dr. Lonnie Mulder, who complained in Capetown at about that very moment that the Montoneros were bent over their shovels and his own black flock were picking the gold out of the wall two miles beneath him, that the BBC was 'in the hands of extremists'?

I see that Judge Sirica, who wants to fly three doctors to California to see if the man who was fit enough to lead the free world just a few weeks ago is fit enough to sit in the Watergate courtroom for a morning, has asked for a ruling on whether the airfares for the three doctors are going to be paid for by the defence or the prosecution. Even as he spoke, farmers at Curtiss, Wisconsin, shot 675 veal calves and threw them into a common grave in a protest against falling meat prices.

Two thousand people a day, says *The Guardian*, are dying in Ethiopia. That's three to a calf.

Never mind. *That's Entertainment!*, the compendium of old MGM film clips, is now set fair to become the world's alltime top grosser, and the creative way ahead lies clear and bright for all of us, even if the Chelsea dustmen are operating a protection racket and only removing the bins of those who cough up a quid every Friday, even if ladies carry gelignite in their handbags, even if cigarettes are to be rationed while vandals drive bulldozers onto our railway lines and a record twenty-seven people were murdered in Chicago on Columbus Day and the Chairman of the Atomic Energy Authority says that the country would be making a grave mistake if it spent 'ridiculous sums to reduce discharges of activity or chances of a modest accident'.

Never mind. We shall sit here in the twilight, you and I, examining the small print of the social contract, while the drunken believers jet to and fro ten miles above us, our doors nailed fast against our black brothers (those, that is, who have not dropped dead from hunger beside our underpriced meat), as football managers come and go outside and national leaders rise, fall, stay, resign, and are trundled from one cemetery to another, and we shall block our ears from the noise of shooting by watching ever more successful compendia of nostalgic rubbish, some of it good (*That's Shakespeare!*) some of it bad (*That's Proust!*), and we shall try to ignore the strontium seeping into our plumbing, choosing instead to doze a little as we sit, waking only to scratch ourselves reflectively with our giant rubber hands.